M. H. Taylor

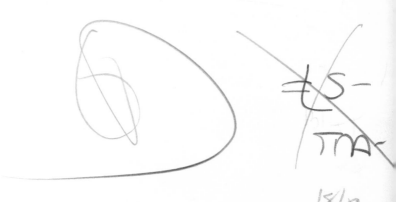

£5-

TTAS

18/20

THE
ROYAL NAVAL SCHOOL
1840–1975

Miss Clifton the First Headmistress
drawn by Dioné Colvile
from an early portrait

THE
ROYAL NAVAL SCHOOL
1840 – 1975

BY

PHILIP UNWIN

★

WITH AN INTRODUCTION BY

Admiral of the Fleet the Earl Mountbatten of Burma
KG, PC, GCB, OM, GCSI, GCIE, GCVO, DSO

The Royal Naval School
Haslemere

First published in 1976

The Royal Naval School, Farnham Lane, Haslemere, Surrey

© *The Royal Naval School 1976*

Printed in Great Britain by
The Longmore Press, Otford, Sevenoaks, Kent

CONTENTS

Page

List of Illustrations 7

Introduction by Admiral of the Fleet The Earl Mountbatten of Burma, KG   9

Author's Note and Acknowledgements 11

Presidents, Chairmen and Headmistresses from 1840 13

  I. THE EARLY YEARS 1840–1854 15

 II. START OF ST. MARGARET'S 1855–1879 26

III. TOWARDS HIGHER STANDARDS 1880–1890 . . . 38

IV. INTO THE NEW CENTURY 1890–1914 50

 V. FIRST WORLD WAR 60

VI. THE TWENTIES 1919–1929 68

VII. THE THIRTIES 1930–1939 80

VIII. SECOND WORLD WAR 1940–1945 93

IX. MID-CENTURY ADVANCE 1946–1960 103

 X. THE LATEST YEARS 1960–1975 115

ILLUSTRATIONS

Between
pages

Frontispiece: Miss Clifton

1 a. Miss Jemima Leys . . . .
  b. Kilmorey St. Margaret's, Twickenham . . . .
  c. Main Hall . . . .
  }
  32-3
2 a. River View at St. Margaret's . . . . . .
  b. 'Canada' Sick Bay . . . .
  c. Hood House . . . .
  d. Gordon House . . . .

3 a. Miss A. E. Chaplin . . . .
  b. Miss W. M. Fayerman . . . .
  c. Dorothea Bluett . . . .
  }
  64-5
4 a. Stoatley Hall front terrace . . . .
  b. Entrance Hall . . . .
  c. Miss Oakley-Hill and Admiral Hall laying stone . . .

5 a. New Kilmorey block . . . .
  b. Art Room . . . .
  c. Domestic Science in action . . . .
  }
  96-7
6 a. Aerial View of Stoatley . . . .
  b. Netball Field . . . .
  c. Cheerful Lacrosse team . . . .

7 a. Mrs. Charlotte McClenaghan with Princess Marina, Earl
     Mountbatten and Admiral Sir John Fleming. . . .
  b. High Rough Sixth Form House . . . . .
  }
  112-3
8 a. Miss Diana Otter with Earl Mountbatten and General Sir Ian
     Riches . . . .
  b. Choir Practice in Kilmorey Hall . . . . . .

7

INTRODUCTION

by

ADMIRAL OF THE FLEET THE EARL MOUNTBATTEN OF BURMA

For the past 20 years I have been proud and honoured to be President of this famous girls' Public School, firstly as a Naval Officer and concurrently since 1965 as the Life Colonel Commandant of the Royal Marines. Tomorrow, 1st January 1976, I hand over the reins to my niece, Princess Anne but do so in the knowledge that on the transfer of Command I am handing over a taut, happy ship of which Her Royal Highness will enjoy being Captain. She is herself the daughter of a Naval Officer and holds the position of Chief Commandant of the WRNS.

Apart from the excellent academic record of the school, its physical situation and appearance might suggest the backing of some rich patron or wealthy foundation. Nothing would be further from the truth. In fact its origin in 1840, under the inspiration of Admirals Sir Thomas Williams and Sir Jaheel Brenton, was a classic example of Victorian self-help devoted to a fine and worthwhile cause.

After the Napoleonic Wars a very large number of Royal Naval and Royal Marine Officers found themselves on half-pay, with little prospect of alternative employment. Many of them were extremely short of money and it was their acute need for an economical means of educating their daughters which gave rise to the idea of the School.

Raising the money entirely by their own efforts, an influential group of mainly Naval and Marine Officers successfully established one of the very earliest girls' boarding schools in England. First it was sited on Richmond Green and then moved to a fine mansion known as 'Kilmorey' on the St. Margaret's site at Twickenham, beside the Thames. This was destroyed by bombing in 1940, fortunately without loss of life.

The difficult moves under wartime conditions, first to Verdley, near Fernhurst and later to Stoatley Hall, were in themselves a triumph of indomitable leadership by a famous Headmistrss, Miss Oakley-Hill. The account of her long reign, including her highly successful post-war developments, occupies a substantial part of the book but it also covers fully the pioneering years in Victorian times – with harsh methods and dull routines unthinkable to a modern generation.

The continuing advances under the various Headmistresses are clearly shown, especially those of Miss Helen Stone who introduced the School to the Twentieth Century and whose work was greatly amplified by her successors, Miss Fayerman who bore the burden of the 1914 war, followed by another great Headmistress, Miss Chaplin who achieved so much in the 1920s and early 1930s.

Indeed the progress and reputation of the school has been largely due to a continuous line of excellent Headmistresses, chosen by a committee of Officers experienced by their profession in picking the right people.

The activities of the school occupy a considerable place in the history of the Royal Navy over the last 135 years, particularly in the welfare field. A good education and a chance in life has been given to thousands of daughters of needy Royal Naval and Royal Marine Officers, especially at times when their future was most bleak; and all this has been done with no financial support other than the donations of the officers themselves and a number of well-wishers.

The spirit of the staff and girls has always impressed me very much. I was greatly intrigued on one visit to discover that some girls were using their own initiative and manufacturing their own cosmetics in the Science Laboratory.

It will be of great interest not only to those connected with the Service in any way, but to all those who share my view that if you firmly believe in what you are doing you will overcome all adversity. The history of the Royal Naval School is a story of great achievement which I hope will prove of some encouragement, particularly in the difficult times we are now facing in our country.

Mountbatten of Burma

A. F.

31st December 1975.

ACKNOWLEDGEMENTS

In the course of an undistinguished academic career which began, curiously enough, in the Kindergarten of a Girls' High School, I did not myself have the privilege of education at the Royal Naval School. For this reason some readers may well be tempted to point out my limitations as its historian.

On the other hand, study of the School records from 1840 to 1975 has given opportunity, one hopes, for a reasonably objective view. The aim has been to tell the story of the origins, rise and development in human and readable terms rather than by exhaustive recital of every known fact.

The task has been made possible only by the continued help and encouragement of General Sir Ian Riches, Rear-Admiral Sir John Fleming and Miss Otter, all of whom read my original typescript and provided helpful suggestions. I am most grateful, also, to:

Mrs. Dioné Colvile who provided line drawings for frontispiece and jacket design; she also gathered many invaluable reminiscences from Old Girls whose letters have done much to recapture the life and atmosphere of the School in earlier days; here, too, the work of Mrs. Thomas and Mrs. Rolfe has been of great assistance.

Among former staff I must acknowledge especially the contribution of Miss Oakley-Hill, extracts from whose Prize Day Reports – as also those of Mrs. McClenaghan – have been a most important source of information, also the memories of Miss A. A. Mowat and Miss Margaret Holbrook. Finally, I would like to thank the present Bursar, Commander James Thomas, for his unfailing readiness to put at my disposal the many documents and records relating the long history of the RNS.

PHILIP UNWIN

Haslemere, 1976

PRESIDENTS, CHAIRMEN AND HEADMISTRESSES FROM THE INCEPTION OF THE SCHOOL IN 1840

PRESIDENTS

1840–41   Admiral Sir Thomas Williams, GCB

1842–60   The Rt. Hon. Earl Manvers

1862–68   Vice-Admiral The Rt. Hon. Earl of Shrewsbury and Talbot, CB

1870–88   Admiral The Hon. Arthur Duncombe

1889–93   Admiral His Royal Highness The Duke of Edinburgh, KG, GCB

1894–1900   H.R.H. The Duke of Saxe-Coburg and Gotha (Duke of Edinburgh, KG)

1901   Rear-Admiral H.R.H. The Duke of Cornwall and York, KG

1902–3   Rear-Admiral H.R.H. The Prince of Wales, KG

1904–6   Vice-Admiral H.R.H. The Prince of Wales, KG

1907–10   Admiral H.R.H. The Prince of Wales, KG

1911   Admiral The Hon. Sir Hedworth Lambton, KCB, KCVO

1912   Admiral The Hon. Sir Hedworth Meux, KCB, KCVO

1913–15   Admiral The Hon. Sir Hedworth Meux, GCB, KCVO

1916–31   Admiral of the Fleet The Hon. Sir Hedworth Meux, GCB, KCVO

1932–36   H.R.H. The Duchess of York

1945–51   H.R.H. The Princess Elizabeth

1955   Admiral The Earl Mountbatten of Burma, KG

1956–75   Admiral of the Fleet The Earl Mountbatten of Burma, KB

CHAIRMEN

1840   Rear-Admiral Sir Jahheel Brenton

1841   Admiral The Right Hon. Sir George Cockburn, GCB

1842   Admiral Sir Charles Rowley, GCB, Bart

1843–47   The Rt. Hon. The Earl Manvers

1848   Rear-Admiral The Rt. Hon. The Earl Walgrave, CB

1849–59   The Rt. Hon. The Earl Manvers

1860–70   Rear-Admiral The Rt. Hon. Lord Colchester

1871   Admiral The Hon. Arthur Duncombe

1872   Captain H.R.H. The Duke of Edinburgh, RN, KG, etc.

1873–79   Admiral The Hon. Arthur Duncombe

1880   Captain The Hon. Fras. Maude, RN

1881–85   Admiral The Hon. Arthur Duncombe

1886   The Rev. J. H. Lang, MA

1887–88   Admiral The Hon. Arthur Duncombe

NOTE : From 1840 to 1888 their was no official Chairman of the Committee. The The names shown above were those who presided as Chairman at the Annual General Meetings. In 1889 the first Chairman of the Committee seems to have been appointed.

1889–94   F. Horatio Fitz-Roy, Esq.

1895   Admiral The Hon. Fras. Egerton

1896–1902   Admiral C. J. Rowley

1903   Rear-Admiral Charles Johnstone

1904–5   Vice-Admiral St. Clair

1906–18   Commander H. F. C. Cavendish, RN

1919–27   Captain H. F. C. Cavendish, RN

1928–29   Admiral Sir William Goodenough, KCB, MVO

1930–31   Admiral Sir Rudolph W. Bentinck, KCB, KCMG

1932–43   Vice-Admiral The Hon. Sir Herbert Meade-Fetherstonhaugh, KCVO, CB, DSO

1944–45   Instructor Rear-Admiral A. E. Hall, CB, CBE

1946–58   Instructor Rear-Admiral Sir Arthur Hall, KBE, CB

1959   Rear-Admiral Sir Philip Clarke, KBE, CB, DSO

1960–65   Instructor Rear-Admiral Sir John Fleming, KBE, DSC, MA

1966–71   Lady Nicholson

1972–   General Sir Ian Riches, KCB, DSO, RM

HEADMISTRESSES

1840–70   Miss Clifton

1871–82   Miss Quinan

1883–1904   Miss Jemima Leys

1905–14   Miss H. G. Stone, BA (London)

1914–20   Miss W. M. Fayerman, Cambridge Mathematical Tripos, Senior Optime

1920–33   Miss A. E. Chaplin, B.Sc. (London)

1933–59   Miss H. M. Oakley-Hill, MA (OXON)

1960–70   Mrs. Charlotte McClenaghan, MA (DUBLIN)

1970–   Miss Diana Otter, BA, AKC, DIP. ED. (OXON)

THE EARLY YEARS

'THE object of the Royal Naval Female School, as established on the 2nd of April, 1840, agreeably to the intention of the Founder, is to bestow upon the daughters of necessitous Naval and Marine Officers, of and above ward-room rank at the lowest reduction of cost practicable, a good, virtuous and religious education, in conformity with the principles and doctrines of the Church of England.'

So reads Paragraph One in the list of 18 Laws drawn up for the management of the School. The severity, not unmixed with the patronage of this language, strikes a strange note to-day. Yet one hundred and thirty-six years ago it stood for a bold and courageous attempt to meet a very serious need in one particular class of society. Greatly as the School has altered and developed over the years and vastly changed as are the qualities of its pupils, one may reasonably feel that the benevolent Founder, Admiral Sir Thomas Williams, were he able to re-visit his creation – granted some understanding of the modern world – would look with admiration and approval upon the achievement of his successors.

He had himself been born so long ago as 1760 and had enjoyed a distinguished career in the Navy of Nelson's time.

It is appropriate to consider, for a moment, the state of England and the conditions of life for women and girls in the year 1840. The young Queen Victoria had been on the throne for only three years, her eldest son, the future King Edward VII, not yet born. Railways were just beginning, for most travellers the horse was essential, otherwise they walked, and though the Navy had experimented with steamships in a very minor way it was still utterly dependent upon sail. Another twelve years were to pass before the first ship-of-the-line was to be a steamer, and she was a wooden vessel fully equipped with sails. Thirty years more were to pass before the first Education Act provided elementary schooling for all, meanwhile even in the middle classes there was little attempt, in the first half of the century, to treat the education of girls seriously. Through much of that prosperous period life could be barren and frustrating for intelligent women. Their situation remained very much as it was in the time of Jane Austen (who incidentally had two brothers in the Navy and much admired the Service). Their thoughts were confined almost wholly to the prospect of marriage with little, if any, consideration of the responsibilities that followed. Even some years later the protest could still be made that girls were not educated to be wives but merely to get husbands; any idea of other serious professions was far ahead.

Queen's College, Harley Street, was yet to come, in 1848, and Bedford College for Women a year later. Miss Frances Buss, born in 1827, opened her North London Collegiate School in 1850, while Miss Dorothea Beale did not begin her distinguished career as Head of Cheltenham Ladies College until 1858, the school itself being founded only in 1854. The famous Girls' Public Day School Trust was not founded until the 1870s and even then their High Schools encountered much opposition from influential quarters, the Duchess of Northumberland protesting that she would 'rather see her daughter at the wash-tub than in a High School'. Girls might learn the piano, drawing and embroidery but nothing too 'taxing' – it was seriously suggested that too much mental effort for them could easily 'lead to the straitjacket'. In 1840 when most girls were taught at home by governess or maiden aunt the very idea of a school for them was a pioneering enterprise.

What inspired Admiral Williams to his decision was the unfortunate situation of so many naval officers after the Napoleonic Wars. The inevitable run-down of the Navy, all too familiar to two generations of sailors in our own time, led to a very large number of them being placed upon half-pay.

So then, to the meeting of senior naval officers which took place at the attractive address of 'The Thatched-House Tavern' in Jermyn Street, London, on Thursday the 2nd day of April 1840, under the chairmanship of Rear-Admiral Sir Jaheel Brenton. It was a distinguished company, many admirals and captains, and the marines were well represented. Their straightforward deliberations, the clear and simple resolutions reached are, in many respects, typical of the direct, self-help achievements of the Victorians and the earliest Report serves to bring alive the spirit of the founders. First there is the moving and forthright statement of Admiral Brenton:

'. . . we cannot hesitate in urging the claim of this proposed Institutic n upon a generous public, in behalf of those whose meek and patient suffering nc ed only to be known to ensure general sympathy; being for the daughters of cfficers, who, having gained their commissions in the Navy by their gallant and faithful services in war, have been left at the peace, on a small pittance of half-pay scarcely adequate in some instances, to procure bread for their children.

'At the termination of the war in 1815, not less than 5000 officers were placed upon the half-pay list; few of them have been called into active service, and many were incapable, from infirmity, of receiving an appointment. It is obvious that an officer of the Navy upon his half-pay – the amount of which is necessarily limited – is utterly incapable of affording such an education to his female children, at least, as might enable them to take their place in the world with a fair prospect of success. . . .

'About ten years ago a school was established for the sons of Naval and Marine Officers . . . but valuable as this school certainly is, it is evident, that, to obtain the means of giving education to female children is of paramount importance; the boy may receive from his father instruction which, with the bold and adventurous character he has inherited, may fit him to rough it in the world. To the daughters no such advantages present themselves – without education to qualify them for the station in life to which they are born, the prospect is indeed gloomy – and their case calls for the support of an Institution, where the want of pecuniary means on the part of the parent may be remedied by public liberality.

'. . . we confidently hope that liberal donations and contributions will flow in from our nobles, our gentry, our merchants and our public bodies, in remembrance that when a world in arms was opposed to us, we were protected and preserved, through the blessing of Divine Providence, upon the gallant exertions of the men for whose offspring we are now pleading.'

The speed at which the Founders went to work was astonishing as was the achievement of the President, Vice-Presidents and Committee. The period might be lacking in those social and educational services which we take for granted to-day, but there was virtually no restriction in regulations or bye-laws to delay the work of an able and determined group of men with a clear and excellent object in view. The success of the first appeal was remarkable: just under 300 people responded, the 'Queen Dowager' heading the list and a munificent £1000 from Admiral Williams being the largest amount. Naval Officers predominated but there were several civilians including a large number of ladies. At the end of the first year the sails had filled out much further, with some 1200 subscribers, the Royal Patronage strengthened by the addition of Queen Victoria herself and there was a far higher proportion of non-naval support. A somewhat touching and extremely impressive footnote to the main list of subscribers recorded that:

'In addition to former contributions the undermentioned Officers have given up a Day's Pay to assist in fitting-up the School House.' There followed thirty-six names and amounts which give us at once their rates of pay: Admiral £1, Captain 10 shillings (50p), Lieutenant 5 shillings (25p). Perhaps they each had daughters but it was, anyhow, typical of the generous actions of navy men at several stages of the School's history.

The Committee quickly drew up its 'Laws' three of which set out plainly the basis of admission:

'Each pupil shall pay £12 per annum in aid of the funds of the Institution; but should the Funds increase, so as to admit a certain number on a still more reduced scale, or even without payment, it shall be in the power of the Managing Committee to receive them on such terms.' The claims for admission were to be founded upon the 'services and circumstances of the father, and the pecuniary situation of the family'. Then followed the Law which would be anathema to modern educationists but which embodied a principle which proved invaluable to the establishment of many charitable organizations in the last century. The precise wording was:

'The mode of admission to the School shall be as follows: The Candidates having been approved by the Committee, the names of those selected shall be submitted to the supporters of the Institution, and admitted by vote; one vote being allowed for every five shillings annual subscription; and doners of two guineas (£2·10p) as life subscribers, to be entitled to one vote, and an additional vote for every two guineas contributed'.

In a third Law, care was taken to ensure that there should be no visible distinction amongst pupils to indicate those who were received at the very lowest rate and those in more fortunate circumstances, for whom higher fees were paid.

An eminently sensible provision in days when the country's banking system was far from universal was that donations could be paid to any of the Navy

B

Agents and to certain officers at the leading naval establishments such as Devonport, Portsmouth, and Weymouth. These few facts are sufficient to indicate the very high level of proficiency in every aspect of the enterprise, basic organization and fund-raising shown by this thirty man committee, all but two of them Naval Officers, whose experience of business matters one imagines might have been limited. We next see the speed with which the School itself came into being, rough and ready perhaps by later standards, but fully 'operational'.

It was fortunate that by the munificence of Admiral Sir Thomas Williams a house on Richmond Green was put at the disposal of the Committee. In his own words: 'I am prepared to take upon myself the entire expense of rent for the first seven years . . . to enable us with safety to launch our vessel tolerably well equipped'.

'Hope House', which was its name, was unfortunately destroyed by fire, in 1856, soon after the School had moved, and though another house was put up on the site little appears to be known of the original. It was in the position now occupied by Onslow Hall next door to the present day Richmond Theatre. One of the earliest prospectuses stated that: 'Parents will be glad to know that only two men, the Doctor and the Chaplain, are allowed over the threshold'.

An early estimate prepared by one of the Committee makes modest provision for 30 pupils at the start and some of the items, with their costs, have an historic interest to-day:

Lady Superintendent	£60 p.a.
3 Teachers	£30, £40 and £45 respectively p.a.
5 Servants	£10–£16 each p.a.
Coals and candles	£80
Books and Stationery	£40
Washing	£120
Medical care	£40

Besides the items mentioned above much else was noted in the first Annual Report in 1841, e.g. 'not only the expense of the necessary alterations and repair of the House, but the laying out of the Playground, also the purchase of all the furniture for the Establishment, including Books, Globes, Piano-fortes, &c.'. Every attention was paid to economy and obviously the furnishing and equipment would have seemed spartan in the extreme to a modern parent, yet it was probably far above that of the boys' Public Schools at the time. Moreover, it was a largely pioneering effort, one of the very first of the girls' Public Schools.

Ladies with the somewhat curious title of 'Vice-Patronesses' were appointed, twelve of them, to visit and inspect the School and report its state occasionally to the Managing Committee but no gentlemen except fathers, guardians or brothers were to visit the School without the express authority of the Committee, or in company with one of the Lady Vice-Patronesses.

In accordance with their Law XVIII which provided that before the business of the meeting 'a Prayer shall be offered up to Almighty God for a blessing upon the same' the Committee were able to record 'no common feelings of gratitude and thankfulness' to Him for the success which attended their labours during their first year.

To this day that Law XVIII is faithfully observed by the Committee. Prayers used are varied, many naval ones have their place naturally, and the work is approached very much in the spirit of the naval tradition typified in the immortal words of Sir Francis Drake:

'O Lord God, when thou givest to us thy servants any great matter, grant us also to know that it is not only the beginning, but the continuing of the same until it be thoroughly finished, which yieldeth the true glory; through him who for the finishing of thy work laid down his life, our Redeemer, Jesus Christ.'

The School was already a going concern and they had been fortunate and wise in their choice of Miss Clifton as Lady Governess (a significant title perhaps with its clear suggestion of the female counterpart of Governor) who was to superintend the tuition and 'direct the internal economy'. Some effort is needed to imagine the weight of responsibility which must have rested upon her shoulders not only teaching but all the work of a modern school bursar, the superintendence of a sizeable domestic staff and a careful eye to the health of young girls in days when such killers as small-pox, scarlet fever and diphtheria were rife.

Beyond stating that after much careful examination on the part of the Vice-Patronesses and the Committee, Miss Clifton, 'a lady fully qualified to undertake the responsible office' was appointed, there is no clue from the early records as to the methods employed. No women could possess university degrees then, there were no professional journals in which such a position could be advertised though, maybe some note in *Times* or *Morning Post* would have brought in suitable applicants, but when they did apply none could have had the exact sort of experience for which a later selection committee would have looked. It reflects well upon the Founders' innate good sense and judgement of character that they were so successful in their first choice.

Many readers will know *The Beth Book* by Sarah Grand, author of a late Victorian best seller *The Heavenly Twins,* and a short section of the former is said to convey an accurate picture of life at the School in years 1867 to 1869. The following quotation leaves no doubt as to the fine qualities of the first Lady Governess, disguised here under the name of Clifford. (Beth is a spirited young girl but is plainly in a difficult stage of her adolescence: the scene is school prayers at the end of her first day)

'The whole household, including the servants, came trooping into the hall . . . Miss Clifford came in, attended by her maids of honour, mounted the reading desk, and read the little service in a beautiful voice devoutly. Beth softened as she listened, and joined in with all her heart towards the end. When prayers were over and the servants had gone downstairs . . . the first-class girls rose and left their seats in single file, and each as she passed walked up to Miss Clifford, took the hand she held out and curtsied good-night to her. The other classes followed in the same order. Miss Clifford said a word or two to some of the girls and had a smile for all. When Beth's turn came, she made an awkward curtsey in imitation of the others. Miss Clifford held her hand a moment, and looked up into her face keenly; then smiled and let her go. Beth felt there was some special thought behind that smile and wondered what it was. Miss Clifford made it her duty to know the character, temper, constitution, and capacity of every one of the eighty girls under her and watched carefully for every change in them. This good-night, which was a dignified and impressive ceremony, gave her an opportunity of inspecting each girl separately every day and very little escaped her. If a girl looked unhappy, run-down, overworked or otherwise out of sorts, Miss Clifford sent for her next morning to find out what was the matter; and she was scolded, comforted, put on extras, had a tonic to take, or was allowed another hour in bed in the morning, according to the necessities of her case.' The real Lady Governess, Miss Clifton, had undoubtedly exceptional talents and qualities of personality which earned her great respect and affection during those thirty years in which she controlled the School.

Forty pupils were at first elected for admission at the £12 scale and a further nineteen were glad to take advantage of the School at the higher scale, making a total of fifty-nine, thus justifying the remark in the first Report, 'That it is a matter of surprise, that it should have been left to the nineteenth century to originate a Royal Naval Female School'. Another point underlining the need for the School comes to light in the fact that five of the first year girls had lost both their parents and fourteen had lost their fathers.

In relation to the number of pupils the size of the teaching staff at the outset appears large by any standard, and it must have compared well with other similar 'institutions' at the time. There were six resident lady teachers, including a Mademoiselle Stinson and visiting 'professors' of Music and of Drawing – just what their actual qualifications were is not stated; courtesy professorships appear then to have been conceded readily! It was however a sound move to get French established in the syllabus at once, to be followed some years later by German. This was well in conformity with one of the rules viz. 'That the education of the pupils do consist of sound and useful knowledge, together with such accomplishments and practice in domestic economy, as may qualify them for whatever situations in society they may be found capable of filling'. The adjoining rule covered this somewhat curious assortment of requirements:

'That each pupil on admission to the School must be provided with a Bible, Prayer-book, Dessert and Tea Spoon, and also pay One Pound, instead of providing Sheets and Towels.' Understandably the religious instruction of all pupils was taken seriously, it was to be 'conducted under clerical supervision, and they shall constantly attend divine service at some approved church in the vicinity unless prevented by illness. . . .' An item in the early accounts of £27 for church 'sittings' is a reminder of a less desirable feature of the times.

However, the religious instruction was undoubtedly successful because, according to a report in the *United Services Gazette* in June 1842 an examination conducted by the local vicar showed most satisfactory results in 'Scripture History and Christian Knowledge, in doctrine and precept'; also included were good exam results in 'Ancient and Modern History, French, Geography,

Chronology, Arithmetic, Orthography, &c., with specimens of Drawing and Needlework, and such exercise in music as time allowed'. The actual methods by which these subjects were taught, and the books used, would perhaps horrify many to-day but the fact still remains that it was surely a considerable achievement in less than two years to have reached this stage. There were then 80 girls and to quote again from the journal 'as in the largest room available for the purpose, many of the visitors could not obtain entrance it has been deemed necessary for the health and prosperity of the Establishment that a sufficiently capacious School room should be erected during the vacation'. An appeal for funds followed and the article concluded 'A visit to the School at Richmond will ensure its recommendation to every benevolent mind'.

Two years had been sufficient to provide the fullest justification for the hopes of the Founders and confirmation of the need for the School. Though obliged to work within a tight budget they had obtained so far, sufficient financial support, and the house on Richmond Green was full to overflowing; fortunately the appeal for funds for the larger room was successful and in 1843 it was reported that 'a new and capacious Schoolroom has been built, thus adding materially to the comfort and convenience of the pupils' (all done within a matter of months). Significantly too, the first baths were fitted and an Infirmary completed. With the former they were probably well in advance of other boarding schools: it is known that many schoolboys – some years later in the century – had to be content with a mere hand-basin in which to wash their feet once a week!

The medical care, also, appears to have been as good as could have been expected at the time. A certain Dr. Julius was the 'Honorary Consulting Physician' and for many years his son *Mr.* F. Julius as 'Honorary Surgeon' – a reminder of the days when many a doctor practised with only his surgical qualification. In due time, however, young Mr. Julius evidently acquired his LRCP, or its equivalent, and is duly described as Doctor, and succeeded his father as Physician to the School. Between them they appear to have done well in their appointment, especially bearing in mind how limited was the armoury against serious infections more than a century ago.

The Committee meanwhile, continued their sound and enterprising policies in financial management. In 1842 a strip of land adjoining Hope House, which had been held by weekly tenants who 'might have become a nuisance', was taken over at the modest rent of £25 p.a. and on this a wash house was put up, thus saving a large part of that formidable item for washing (£120) mentioned in the original estimate. Also, particularly pleasant before a playing field existed, there was sufficient spare ground available for each pupil to have a little garden to cultivate.

Such had been the success of the various appeals made both in Naval circles and elsewhere that the income for the year had been just equal to expenditure but this was due only to the substantial number of 'subscriptions'. Fifty-four pupils were paying only the minimum though the cost was not under £31.10s. per annum. Also after Midsummer 1847, the rent of the house would have to be paid out of the ordinary income, as the seven years for which the Founder had provided for that object, would then have expired. The death of Admiral Sir Thomas Williams had been noted with great regret in the previous year and arrangements made for a portrait of him by Frederick Say to hang in the School.

A wise provision made by the Founder ensured that only the annual subscriptions could be used as income, all donations and Payments made as Life Subscriptions were to go into an invested fund which, after three years had reached the very respectable total of £3000, all invested in Consols yielding only 3 % but in those far off days certain to hold their value. While this fund was to grow steadily over the years it was the regular payments from the subscribers, numbering nearly 3000 in the 1860s, which provided almost half the running expenses, the rest made up by the fees of the pupils. After ten years or so, a few of the City Livery Companies were responding with useful three-figure sums, and like amounts came from a very small number of wealthy patrons but the vast proportion was made up of two and five 'guinea' subscriptions – many from ladies, obviously keen to give the girls a chance – and frequently several members of the same family. It amounted to a wonderfully wide spread of support and makes one think again, with some humility, of the energy and, not infrequently the self-denial, with which many Victorians responded to a cause of this nature.

Before leaving financial matters it must be mentioned that the School, too, did its best by keeping pigs to feed upon the inevitable scraps from so large a household. An item in the early accounts records 'Profit from pigs' £21 (well over £300 to-day) also, a little mysteriously, 'sale of bones £3'. On an entirely different level of money-raising, the Duchess of Mulgrave composed an anthem upon the 107th Psalm, had it published and then gave the proceeds of £14 to the School.

That was in 1846 and it was not until that year that the railway to Richmond opened from the point later to be known as Clapham Junction. A further example of the speed of work then, long before man possessed earth-moving machinery, is that the line was completed in only nine months, cuttings and bridges included. There had been 98 omnibuses daily between Richmond and London previously so that it had been by no means out of touch even before the line came, but thereafter the town must have grown more rapidly.

At this time the application form for the admission of pupils makes interesting reading; doubtless the fruit of experience in running the School, it was searching in its questions and ensured that no unduly dull child was accepted or that her family had unsuspected sources of income. Her actual attainments in those now oft neglected 'Three R's' had to be stated and her 'progress in other branches'. On health, an inevitable period touch was the question whether vaccinated or had had small-pox, and number of brothers and sisters *living*. The 'Pecuniary Situation of Applicant' left no loop-hole, questioning 'Full or Half Pay, Pension, R.N. Benevolent Society, Income from Private Property or Property left in trust for Wife or Children and any other source of income'. Seemingly a tough means test but completely fair in the circumstances and it was allied to generous waiving of rules in certain cases of extreme need.

As there was little change in the number of the staff in the late 1840s it is probable that the curriculum did not alter greatly and the girls' daily routine would have appeared dull and little short of Draconian in many respects; organized games on a proper playing field were still some years ahead. Already, however, there was good evidence that the first great object was being achieved, as many letters from parents gave 'pleasing evidence that the Institution is held in high esteem'. One father wrote: 'I have every reason to be satisfied with the many benefits my daughter has gained at your valuable Institution, not only in scholarly acquirements but what is of more value than these, in moral culture and religious instruction. I have . . . long observed the mental improvement of my daughter . . . a solid foundation for all that is valuable in female education has now been laid'. A mother, after learning that her daughter had to leave on attaining the age of 18 wrote: 'Many a widowed mother, I doubt not, is ready to bear testimony with me to the consolation it affords to know, in the event of her death, their children will be able to provide for themselves when thus educated'.

The poignant note in the latter can be well understood. With no prospect of Old Age pensions or 'supplementary allowances' the outlook for an unmarried and relatively uneducated woman could be bleak indeed if left unprovided for by her parents. Other letters mentioned the satisfaction at the posts, as governesses and teachers, which were secured by some of the girls after they left; others, again proved a great help to their parents in relieving them of some of the burden of the junior members of large families. Some may well regard this as 'small beer' in terms of professions for women but it was very much a step in the right direction; here was some small chance of independence, and in another generation it was to lead on to much wider opportunities. In less than ten years the reputation of the School had become such that the fact of a girl having been a satisfactory pupil there became, in itself, 'a sufficient recommendation to secure engagements for those qualified for, and desirous to get out in life as governesses'.

While some might have had a difficult time, in their mid-way status between family and servants in a large household probably most governesses would have found fulfilment and interest in the work. One supposes that the type of young lady produced by the R.N. Female School would have been in the latter category. In the end, moreover, those who would thus get out in life must have had a better chance of marriage. By the 1850s there was particularly gratifying news that one of the earliest pupils had been offered an appointment in India 'to organize and superintend the education of Native Female Teachers'. The outcome was not reported, one hopes that the courageous young woman's health stood up to what was then a severe test, but it was a fine testimony to her old school.

A few years later a gentleman in whose family a former pupil was governess wrote:

'Miss H--- lived 8 years in my family, having the charge of four children; my eldest daughter afterwards accompanied her to Hanover. It is not easy to express my approbation of her services, or the high estimate I entertain of her character; with talents of the highest order, it is not surprising that my children reaped immense advantages from her tuition, and that my boys were able to rank in schools with boys beyond their own age. Knowing that there is ordinarily some disadvantage in boys of ten years of age remaining in charge of a lady, they were examined by the Master of one of our leading Grammar Schools who found them so well grounded as to advise their continuance with Miss H---. One of my boys, now 13 years of age, is in a school devoted to preparation for Eton and Harrow, and is second amongst forty boys, many of them his seniors'. Granted that this boy may have been a natural genius, and Miss H--- an exceptional young woman, it still remains an impressive account, and added to the earlier evidence of the success of other girls in teaching does surely indicate that St. Margaret's was doing good work despite some shortcomings, described later.

A glance at the Navy at this point reminds us that whilst it remained still one of sailing ships, the development of screw propulsion had made steam of greater potential value to a warship because there was no longer so much vital space amidships monopolised by the paddleboxes. At sea, the engineer was becoming recognized as a man of importance and in the Report of 1849 the Committee included the historically interesting statement that 'In accordance with the regulations of the Admiralty . . . such naval engineers as hold wardroom rank are recognized as entitled to avail themselves of all the privileges of the School'. The steam engine with its inevitable smoke and dirt had not been welcomed by officers accustomed to the spotless decks of a sailing ship and it is small wonder that there was an initial reluctance to accept, as one of themselves, this new breed of men – vital though their contribution was to become in the future. It is good to know that the School authorities quickly moved with the times in this matter.

Simultaneously there came an important advance in domestic convenience: it was considered advisable to have the School lit by gas and the Directors of the Richmond Gas Company 'liberally contributed 20 per cent of the entire outlay'. Probably much of it was in the form of the plain 'fish-tail' burner – before the incandescent gas-mantle became general – but in place of the scores of candles and oil lamps (having to be trimmed daily) it must have come as an enormous boon and a great saving of labour – to say nothing of the much greater safety. Also in the same report is the interesting confirmation that the good Dr. Julius and his son had given 'their professional kindness and skill' freely to the School since its foundation, and the daughter of Mr. F. Julius was to be 'at liberty to attend the School as a day pupil' the inference being that she was taken free. A pleasant gesture towards the Honorary Surgeon who was to give invaluable service over very many years. He had only recently vaccinated every member of the School without cost when a single case of small-pox had been discovered.

In 1852 came the enterprising appointment of a teacher of German and there was an extra charge, at the rate of £3 per annum, for those pupils receiving lessons. It would be interesting to know just how this came about: there must then have been comparatively few schools which would have offered this second modern language. The strong German influence at Court through the Prince Consort might well have been a factor. However, knowledge of German and the ability to teach it was clearly seen by the School as a most useful accomplishment for its embryo governesses. One cannot help reflecting that the language master, Herr Schwitzlein, was not exactly over-paid at £12.15s. per annum; even if the good man put in only one hour a week that would be about 30p. per lesson. It was plainly a good bargain for the School since they required but four girls to take the subject (at £3 each) to cover the cost! One must, of course, remember that a great many zealous Germans were ready then to come here, to work for a pittance, in order to perfect their English and to learn all they could of the country which, in the 19th century, led the world.

In 1854 the subjects taught were:

English	including Writing, Arithmetic, Geography, etc.
French	by a resident French teacher and the attendance of a French Master
Music	by resident Music Teachers and attendance of a Master
Drawing *Singing* *German* *Deportment*	all by visiting teachers

The extremely uncertain nature then of primary teaching is clear from the fact that the Committee felt it 'necessary again to draw attention of the parents of Candidates to the necessity of Pupils being fully prepared by previous training to avail themselves of the educational advantages given at the School. More than one instance has occurred where early education has been so little attended to, that it became a matter for serious consideration whether the pupils could be allowed to remain in the Institution beyond the probationary six months'.

This 1854 Report concluded with a sombre reference to the Crimean War which had just begun, pointing out that many daughters of Naval Officers might be made fatherless as a result and that 'it cannot fail to be a source of consolation to their brethren that in such an event The Royal Naval Female School . . . may be privileged to soothe the sorrows of the widow and orphan, and in some degree repair the loss they will have sustained by the death of a loved husband and honoured father'. One can be sure that these were no empty words and that great efforts would have been made to assist those whose financial situation, for example, might suddenly be worsened.

The war brought another considerable problem for the School. The need for more space was becoming urgent both in, and out, of doors. The period of free rent at Hope House, on Richmond Green, so generously arranged by Admiral Williams, had long since expired and the building itself though invaluable for the start, was not adequate for the growing School and probably did not lend itself to enlargement. The inevitable 'tightness' of money at the start of a war was a far from ideal time for a major public appeal for a new building fund, yet just at that moment an apparently ideal property came on to the market. The full story of it belongs to the next Chapter.

CHAPTER II

START OF ST. MARGARET'S

THE tempting property was the newly built mansion of the eccentric Second Earl of Kilmorey, at St. Margaret's, Isleworth, on the bank of the Thames. He was a most remarkable character. Throughout his long life of 93 years he prided himself on his physical fitness and once, for a wager, he rowed in a four-oared boat (no out-riggers) from Oxford to Westminster Bridge in 14 hours. His greatest interest was the purchase, alteration and improvement of large houses of which, at various times, he owned six different ones, all near the river.

This new house replaced an earlier one, barely thirty years old, which was demolished to make way for the new, designed by Lewis Vulliamy, an architect of some distinction who had done the original Dorchester House in Park Lane. The new one at St. Margaret's was erected by W. Cubitt & Co., leading builders of the time, at a cost then of just under £17,000.

As photographs show, it was a most handsome building. Of rectangular shape, it measured 154 by 57 feet, it was faced by a light-coloured brick with red brick dressings and the imposing Doric portico of the main entrance was in Portland stone. The interior fully lived up to the splendour of the outside and the main staircase was a particularly fine feature with its broad but shallow steps, and the elaborately decorated iron balusters so often found in expensive houses of the period.

There were well matured trees in the grounds which stretched towards the river bank and in the distance, on the opposite bank, were the pleasant houses of Richmond Hill. The general situation was delightful in many respects even though it could be damp and cold in winter. At the time the gross inadequacy of the sanitary arrangements, including drainage direct into the river, would not have caused anxiety though it posed a most serious problem nearly thirty years later.

The extraordinary feature was that the noble Lord ran short of money and was never able to live in the house himself. He sold it – presumably at a loss, to the Conservative Land Society in 1854, and then it was apparently offered to the School. Their Building Fund, after a special appeal, did not reach more than £1,934. Fearing to incur too large a debt, the Committee decided not to proceed and felt in honour bound to offer their money back to the subscribers. Mercifully most of them had sufficient belief in the future to refuse, and before long the Building Fund had grown to £3,000. Meanwhile appropriate steps were taken to make it widely known that only cash shortage had necessitated the School refusing the attractive offer of St. Margaret's for £9,700. In June 1856 (again to quote the Report) 'the Commissioners of the Patriotic Fund were pleased to make a grant of *£5000* to the Society . . . coupled with the condition that the Royal Commissioners shall have the right (in perpetuity) of keeping five pupils in the School, each of these pupils paying £10 each towards their board and education'. It appears that though the actual formalities were not completed until later, there was a sufficient 'understanding' with the Patriotic Fund to enable the School to proceed with their plans.

Promptly the Committee reopened negotiations with the Conservative Land Society purchasing the new house for the sum already mentioned and they successfully sub-let Hope House at Richmond to the Cavalry College. Soon after the latter took possession, a part of the building was accidently burnt down but the School suffered no 'pecuniary loss'. So, in September 1856, the Crimean War notwithstanding, they acquired the very fine new premises with which they were to be identified for the next 84 years.

The actual move from Hope House, Richmond to the new home at St. Margaret's was accomplished during the summer holidays of 1856 and the School was established there for the new term in September. One regrets that there is no record as to how it was all done or how long it took. The horse-drawn, box-like pantechnicons of those days must have rumbled to and fro many times and doubtless those servants of the School, including perhaps some of the resident mistresses, must have worked hard to get all the equipment, desks, 'globes', pianos, books, etc. into place. It seems probable that in the absence of any large fund for extra furniture, the bigger house must have seemed rather bare but the beauty of its situation would have been compensation enough. Efforts to raise extra donations for the cost of the house had been remarkably successful and the new regime began with a deficit of no more than a few hundred pounds on the total of nearly £10,000 which had been required. Evidence of the already wide reputation and appeal of the Royal Naval Female School is clear from the list of contributors which extends from 'Profits of an Amateur Performance given at the request of the Queen £180', to many members of the aristocracy, great bankers such as Baring Brothers, Coutts, Williams Deacon, all £100 each, and – curiously – 'Mr. Whampoa, a well known merchant of Singapore'.

Apart from this special outlay which, of course, provided a most valuable freehold asset, the Committee adhered firmly to the directive of the Founder that all donations as distinct from subscriptions should be used to build up the endowment fund and two years after the move they could most properly announce that a further £800 had been invested in the worthy Consols.

One effect of the move had been to put them too far away for the girls easily to attend their former church and there was no other within walking distance. Services were held in the School Hall and after a time an astute arrangement was arrived at: the Rev. R. F. Wheeler was appointed as their chaplain at a stipend 'not exceeding the amount formerly paid by the School in pew rents'.

Some years were yet to pass before the School was able to build its own quite pleasant chapel in the grounds, a stone Victorian gothic structure with orna-mental brick interior and fitted pews, very much in the accepted style of the times. A note in the accounts of 1871 reveals an expenditure of £33 for warming apparatus in the chapel which leads one to suppose that it had been virtually unheated during the early years of its use. This comes as yet another reminder of the tough, and in many respects seemingly comfortless, life endured by children a century ago.

Before considering the daily routine then, of the little Royal Naval Females one has to remember that in the view of kindly, well-disposed Victorians (the writer had one such respected great-uncle who was venerated by his eleven children) the young were creatures who *had* to obey their elders; they were as young horses whose insolent spirits must be broken-in, to accustom them to the 'harness' of the world. Such views would shock most people now but, as well as some casualties, the period produced many fine men and women and who shall say that other methods in the present day do not produce their casualties? This is no place for a dissertation upon discipline and education; the point is touched upon merely to remind the reader that the regime described below, and further on, would have been customary for a large proportion of middle class boys and girls at that time.

The Beth Book, mentioned earlier, leaves no doubt as to the reputation for strictness at what is disguised as 'St. Catherine's Mansion, the Royal Service School for Officers Daughters'. The heroine's arrival and her first few hours tell their story:

'. . . the house was beautiful and so also were the grounds about it, and the view of the river, the bridge with its many arches and the grey town climbing up from it. Beth was standing under the steps, under the great portico, where her mother had left her, contemplating the river which was the first that had flowed into her experience.

'Come, come, my dear, come in, you are not allowed to stand there'. Beth turned and saw a thin, dry, middle aged woman with a sharp manner . . . and behind her a gentler looking lady, who said, 'It is a new girl, Miss Bey. I expect she is all bewildered.'

'No, I am not at all bewildered, thank you' Beth answered in her easy way.

'Then you had better come at once', Miss Bey rejoined drily, 'and let me see what you can do. Please remember in future that the girls are not allowed to come to this door.' (She led the way upstairs to a narrow class-room.)

'What arithmetic have you done?' Miss Bey began.

'I've scrambled through the first four rules', Beth answered.

'Set yourself a sum in each and do it', Miss Bey said sharply.

When the sums were done Miss Bey took the slate and glanced at them. 'They are every one wrong', she said, 'but I see you know how to work them. Now clean the slate and do some dictation.'

She took up a book when Beth was ready and began to read aloud from it. Beth became so interested in the subject that she forgot the dictation and burst out at last, 'Well, I never knew that before'.

'You are doing dictation now', Miss Bey observed severely.

'All right, go on', Beth cheerfully rejoined.

'May I ask what your name is?' Miss Bey inquired.

'Beth Caldwell.'

'Then allow me to inform you, Miss Beth Caldwell, that "all right, go on" is not the proper way to address the headmistress of the Royal Service School for Officers' Daughters.'

'Thank you for telling me', Beth answered. 'You see I don't know these things . . .'

'Have you ever been to school before?' Miss Bey asked.

'No', said Beth.

'Oh', Miss Bey ejaculated with peculiar meaning. 'Then you will have a great deal to learn.'

'I suppose so', Beth rejoined. 'But that's what I came for, you know – to learn. It's high time I began!' She fixed her eyes on the blank wall opposite, and there was a sorrowful expression in them. Miss Bey noted the expression, and nodded her head several times, but there was no relaxation of her peremptory manner when she spoke again. (Later, though, she and Beth got on good terms.)

In fact Beth proves to be too much a high spirited individualist to settle into the rigid routine and her lack of earlier schooling puts her at a disadvantage in many subjects. Yet, at the same time, her lively inquiring mind finds most of the lessons dull and unimaginative. The resultant depression prevents her from enjoying her marked ability in piano playing and English composition which do nevertheless impress some of her teachers. She makes few friends and is, obviously for the staff, a 'difficult' girl. However, the author's undoubted regard for the Lady Governess (in reality Miss Clifton) is clear from the words put into her mouth when replying to another mistress on the subject of Beth: 'Well, be patient with her, if she hasn't exceptional ability of some kind, I am no judge of girls; but she is evidently unaccustomed to school work, and is suffering from the routine and restraint, after being allowed to run wild. She should have been sent here years ago.'

The 'Miss Clifford' of the book shows her further wisdom over Beth by finally advising her mother to remove her to another school, as it is clear that her health is suffering from her sense of frustration and confinement. Thus her credit at the 'Royal Service School' was saved by the good judgement of a 'kind and wise woman' and her career there ended honourably, if somewhat abruptly.

High as was the author's opinion of the Principal, she was certainly most critical of much of the school routine, blaming it partly upon the 'dowager-persons' (supposedly the Vice-Patronesses?) who 'used their influence strenuously to make the life there as much a punishment as possible'. Because many of the girls were orphans without means and would therefore have to earn their own living as governesses, it was thought that 'you cannot be too strict with girls in their position . . . the result was the girls were deprived of every innocent pleasure natural to their age and necessary to their health and spirits. They had no outdoor games at all, not even croquet – nothing whatever to exhilarate them and develop them physically except an hour's deportment . . . once a fortnight.'

There were, of course, the inevitable afternoon walks, strictly supervised formal affairs when the girls proceeded two-by-two in crocodile formation through the mainly residential neighbourhood. It was some form of exercise in fresh air but was scarcely lively or stimulating.

Obviously there was a great deal which a modern mind must criticize in the apparent outlook of those Vice-Patronesses but one must view them in the climate of their time. To its shame, the Victorian age did tend to look down upon women who were obliged to work for their living; those responsible for the running of the School were engaged on an undertaking which had a considerable element of 'charity' in it and they had to exercise the greatest care in the spending of money which had been voluntarily contributed by so many individuals, many of them far from well-off. When all is said and done, the Committee had, as we have seen, set the School firmly on its feet and built up a good reputation for carrying out the work for which it was intended. Methods of teaching for girls were to be revolutionised in the latter part of the 19th century and the Royal Naval School was to move ahead with them.

Lest it be thought that the St. Margaret's standards were unduly exacting, it is interesting to find at the start of Milton Mount College, founded in the 1870s for the daughters of Congregational Ministers, the following statement was made: 'We aim to establish an institution which shall be the opposite of a fashionable boarding school. We wish to give . . . a solid and thorough education to train pupils to love unselfish work and Christian virtues, to honour labour and to cultivate independence of feeling', and on the opening day the head-mistress announced that 'no prizes would be given. The luxury of acquiring knowledge is its own reward.'

Though many years were to pass before prizes were given at St. Margaret's, Speech Day was already inaugurated and a report of one in 1867 makes good reading. It appeared in the *Middlesex Chronicle* and the core of the occasion was the half-yearly examination of the pupils, done before a distinguished company of visitors, and involving, one would have thought, an appalling strain for both teachers and the girls. However, the account tells us:

'The 85 pupils in their summer costume and glowing with healthy excitement, formed a pleasing portion of what was really a charming picture. Of course the majority of those present were sailors for the the young ladies are daughters of the sea. The proceedings of the day opened with prayer and the beautiful hymn *Ye Saints and Servants of the Lord* . . . at its conclusion Mr. Hales examined the the pupils upon the Scriptures and the replies he received were given with a readiness which proved careful training. . . . The music by ten performers upon as many pianos, which followed, was listened to with an amount of attention not always bestowed by a fashionable audience (it seems well nigh unbelievable, but they did have all those pianos in one room, according to Beth!). At its conclusion a German master examined the young ladies of the first class . . . the replies, given without the slightest hesitation, were noted by the teachers with anxious interest, this branch of instruction being a prominent feature at this Institution.' A similar examination in French followed, then the repetition of a scene from Racine's *Esther* 'with a purity of accent and fervour of manner . . .

not often heard in a scholastic establishment'. Examination in the Theory of Music, by a Dr. Selle followed – this based upon the printed form of The College of Preceptors – then came an astonishing achievement, the performance of the overture to Weber's *Euryanthe* by twenty performers upon ten pianos to the entire satisfaction of Dr. Selle, who was one of the first to express unqualified approval . . . the music mistress glancing at her pupils with a look of pardonable pride . . . Dr. Schneider now examined the second class in German and the glowing cheerful face of the youngest child, as she replied, was good to look upon'. The Hon. Captain Maude, then the Secretary to the School, wound up the proceedings and 'with marked emphasis specially dwelling upon the loving able services of Her whose heart is mother to them all, Miss Clifton, who has just entered her 27th year of duties, the mention of whose name being hailed with loud applause by all present, from the youngest child to the grey-haired admiral'.

At the end of all this the visitors were entertained to lunch in the sitting room of the Lady Governess (but there is no mention of any particular treat for the girls).

The Report of 1871 notes the successful appointment of a new Lady Governess, Miss Quinan, and her 'zealous performance of her important duties'. She was unfortunate to run into a 'visitation of scarlatina and other ailments' also the sad death of a pupil 'by a sudden and severe attack of inflammation' during her first year of office. Miss Quinan was to achieve much for the School during her 13 years and her position must have developed greatly from that of her predecessor. Yet it seems doubtful whether, with her somewhat imperious manner, she enjoyed the measure of affection which was given to Miss Clifton. The latter had retired in 1870 after 30 years of devoted service, and she was granted a pension, at first of £93 15s., raised after two years to £125. Lest it be assumed too readily that the Committee was exercising undue economy, it must be mentioned that very few jobs were pensionable then; this pension was doubtless non-contributory and the figure should be multiplied by about twenty to give any impression as to its purchasing power today. In fact the kind Miss Clifton enjoyed retirement into her ninetieth year.

Evidence of the increasing status of the School in Service circles by the 1870s appears in the fact that the Annual General Meeting of the Subscribers and Friends now took place at the Royal United Service Institution in Whitehall Yard (probably the 'Thatched House Tavern' had been long since demolished in the course of the massive re-building of London in the last century). Also the number of those attending had doubtless increased. Royal Patronage had been strengthened with 'Captain the Duke of Edinburgh' as well as Queen Victoria; there were 17 Vice-Presidents and an equal number of Vice-Patronesses backed up by an all-male Committee of 29, most of them Admirals and Captains. Together they must have had a wide circle of influential friends and contacts and this probably accounts for the increasing number of legacies and donations reported, also the three scholarships by then in existence. Incidentally, for the investor, it is interesting to observe that whereas railways scarcely existed at the beginning of our story, the Great Northern of England and the East India

Railway were seen as safe investments for the scholarship funds – where security, above all would be sought.

By 1872 a reminder of the advance of steam in the Navy shows, in a list of the fathers' ranks, with nine engineers among a total of 89. Still a preponderance of ships carried sail but the revolutionary change was well on the way. Appropriately there was at the same time a major advance in the teaching policy of the School. In the previous year girls had been examined – for some odd reason at very short notice – by one of the Cambridge Local Examiners and the results were such as to determine the Committee to have the Cambridge Examinations annually, before the summer holidays. This was clear evidence that the academic standard was, at least, up to average and the School was determined to keep it so. At the same time it was emphasised again that pupils admitted must be able to pass the appropriate entrance examination for their age. There had been indications in earlier Reports that some girls had been inadequately prepared and presumably the School had stretched a point in their favour. Now it was pointed out strongly that 'it is as necessary for the benefit of the pupils as well for the character and the well being of the School, that they should be fitted by previous training and preparation to reap the advantages which the Institution affords, as it must be evident that the admission of numerous very backward pupils will seriously delay the progress of others'.

Here are particulars of what was expected at the different ages of admission:

For pupils under 12 years
English – Must read and write fairly from dictation from the 2nd Reading Book of the Society for Promoting Christian Knowledge, 10 lines without making 5 mistakes.
Must know the outlines of Biblical and English History from Pinnock's Catechism.
Arithmetic – Must know the first four rules.
No foreign language obligatory but credit given for proficiency if candidates wish to be examined in French or German.

For pupils under $13\frac{1}{2}$ years
English – as above but from S.P.C.K. Standard III book, 15 lines without making 7 mistakes. Must possess fair knowledge of the principal events recorded in the books of Moses and the four Gospels; also of the principal events of English History from Pinnock's Catechism.
Arithmetic – First 4 Rules Simple and Compound (money only).
Grammar – not obligatory but credit given for being able to distinguish parts of speech in a short sentence.
Geography – Must have an acquaintance with definitions such as Island, Isthmus, Cape, &c. with the names and positions of the Oceans and Continents.
French or German – Must be able to conjugate the two auxiliary verbs 'Avoir' and 'Etre' or 'Haben' and 'Sein'.

For pupils under 15 years
English – As above but from S.P.C.K. Standard IV book. Must have

a

a. Miss Jemima Leys, Headmistress,
   1883–1904.

b. The handsome Kilmorey House,
   St. Margaret's.

c. Part of the original Assembly Hall
   (note pillars at left).

b

c

ST. MARGARET'S,
TWICKENHAM.

a

The beautiful river view from the roof
of Kilmorey.

'Canada' – the Sick Bay.

Hood House.

Gordon House.

good knowledge of historical books of Old Testament up to the Psalms, and Gospels and Acts of the Apostles.
Also English History from William and Mary . . .
Arithmetic – Tables of Weights and Measures, Reduction and Practice.
Grammar – Must be able to parse an easy sentence.
Geography – Must also have an acquaintance with names of principal countries of Old and New Worlds, their principal Rivers and Mountains.
French or German – Must know the four conjugations of verbs in French or the regular verbs in German.

There may be much there which would surprise a modern girl and some that her teachers would regard as useless lumber but it does suggest that the successful candidates did indeed require to have their wits about them and to have had a good grounding by Victorian standards (how some of their great-grand-daughters would have fared at the hands of 'Miss Bey' one is left speculating!)

All too familiar to present-day readers, appears in 1873 a complaint of the great advance in the price of coals and meat and some other articles; it is expected that this tendency will continue and yet again the Committee appeal to the friends of the School and to the public generally for additional support, especially as many of those who contributed regularly in the past 'are fast passing away'. It needed a continual effort to keep the accounts balanced. At the same time they changed the system to *Three Terms* in the course of the year, to bring the School more into harmony with others of similar size, instead of the former arrangement of *Quarters*. One would suppose that the new plan also effected some economies.

At this time there was another change which brought them more into line with modern practice. The formal reign of the Julius family as Honorary Surgeons came to an end after more than 30 years, though Dr. Frederick remained as 'Honorary Consulting Physician'. 'Messrs' Bateman and Fenn (who were nevertheless M.D.s) were appointed as Medical Attendants at a salary of 50 guineas (£52.50). A high opinion was soon formed of their 'kind and unremitting services' and they did indeed act with great efficiency and promptness during a most serious outbreak of scarlet fever some years later.

In the following year, 1874, the rise in prices necessitated, at length, an increase in fees from £40 to £50 per annum, at which the School was still extremely good value, though the 25 % addition must have been a burden for many parents. On the matter of fees, it is interesting to compare one of the most famous of all girls' schools, Cheltenham Ladies' College, which in the 1880s charged approximately £70 a year for boarding and tuition under 15 years of age.

One is aware, also, of an effect of the long period of peace in that the Committee refers to the reduced number of Naval Officers – doubtless one effect of Gladstonian government. Ironically enough, it was all part of the *Pax Britannica* in which the Navy itself played so large a part. Thus there were actually fewer Officers to support the School but this did not prevent the Committee from observing pointedly that 'there are still in the Service many who are not on the list of contributors, whose means certainly would enable them to lend a helping

c

hand to an Institution which for more than 30 years has conferred no ordinary boon on the Service'.

Other details which help to fill in the life at the School, and the problems of the Committee, are that in spite of the warning about the need for parents to see that their daughters were adequately prepared there arose the painful necessity to ask for two girls to be withdrawn, as not up to the required standard, two in 1876, and three in 1877. Happily there were none the following year and the position improved generally. Every opportunity seems to have been given to the candidates because they were allowed a second chance provided there were sufficient vacancies. Among the arithmetical conundrums then offered to candidates were such delights as 'Reduce 613 guineas to farthings' and 'multiply 86 lbs. 7 oz. 16 dwt. 11 grs. by 8' . . . not difficult if you had been taught the method but hopeless if you had not been properly prepared. The total number of the teaching staff, including visiting masters and mistresses, was 16 with the Lady Governess, which may be considered a good provision for not more than 90 girls.

On a purely domestic note, the earlier request that pupils should bring some cutlery with them had been withdrawn and the rules clearly stated no silver spoons, forks, school books or music need be brought, which must have been a relief to many a hard-pressed parent or guardian. Lady Vice-Patronesses having decided in 1876 to meet only once a term, instead of monthly, reverted the following year to the regular monthly meetings. One cannot help speculating as to the need for such frequent inspections now that the School was so firmly established and nearing the end of its fourth decade, it would be interesting also to know how far the Lady Governess welcomed them in conditions so very different from those of the first pioneering years.

The apparent cost of 'board' for a girl in those days is shown by an item in the rules which states that where a pupil cannot go home for Christmas holiday she may remain at the School for the payment of £1 10s. The period must have been at least two weeks and costs of food then for a group would have been reasonably covered at 15 shillings (75p) a head per week but one does wonder what on earth happened to them while, presumably, the teaching staff were away? Life could have been intolerably dull and lonely in that great empty house beside the river in mid-winter unless some friend of the School made a point of entertaining them. (At that stage the School Library was negligible – in Beth's words 'suited only to the capacities of infants and imbeciles'.)

Unless anyone might consider that the Committee showed an undue spirit of economy in management it must be emphasised that, for all the generosity of the many subscribers in Naval circles and elsewhere, the 'Institution' was running on an extremely narrow margin. It was an exceptional year when they managed to show a small balance of receipts over expenditure; not infrequently they had to dip into their reserves for any unusual item, or to make up a small deficit, but continually there is a strong sense of sturdy self-reliance coming through in the Reports – always coupled with that true reliance on Almighty God to bless the work in the value of which they had total confidence.

There was, of course, then no question of any Government grants and the money never *poured in* but subscribers continued their support – though death was reducing the number of the original ones – some legacies came their way, the increase in fees helped and one way and another, by their own efforts, the Committee had just enough to meet their needs.

By 1877 they decided that it was desirable 'as an encouragement to industry – to expend a certain sum every year in the purchase of suitable books as prizes, and they hope that an ample return for the outlay will be seen in a healthy emulation which they trust will be fostered among the pupils'. A somewhat costive way of expressing themselves, some might think, but at least it was the suggestion of a carrot after what had probably been a good deal of 'stick' and the first distribution of prizes took place in the classic month of July by the Dowager Duchess of Northumberland, when 15 were given, a certain Miss Gillies carrying off 5 of them (Literature, French, German, Music and Singing). One longs to know what books were considered suitable where, formerly, Tennyson had been regarded as too advanced even for senior girls. Still, it was a good step forward in providing some excitement and change of routine – and, dare one hope, something nice for tea – at least once in the year?

The total number of teaching staff remained constant though it is remarkable that at one stage all of the non-resident ones were men, including those responsible for, English Literature, Music, German, Latin, Arithmetic, French, Drawing and Drill, though the latter appears to have given way later to Deportment taught by a mistress.

A year later there was a 'prevalence of scarlet fever in the neighbourhood' (often fatal then for children) and the summer holidays were extended by a fortnight. The School escaped any infection but once more came the sad and deplored loss of one of the younger girls who died after a few days' illness notwithstanding 'the great care and medical attention she received'. The death of a child was commonplace then, but one cannot help wondering what were these ghastly 'virus' infections which could carry them off so suddenly? – and spare some thanks for the enormous benefits of anti-biotics and the inoculations of today.

By modern standards there could have been serious deficiencies in their diet, in which bread and butter and weak tea comprised two of the main meals. Milk could not then have been tuberculin-tested and much of it, anyhow, was probably served boiled which would have destroyed most of its nourishment. The science of vitamins was unknown and except for a short time in the year, little fruit would have been available, while, in the custom of the times, most of the goodness of green vegetables was boiled out of them, to leave that soggy mess so detested by past generations of children! Once again one cannot blame the School unduly – such a diet was common to most English children until the present century – but it perhaps offers some explanation why in some circumstances their resistance to disease was not greater.

Meanwhile it was observed that 'every attention is paid to the sanitary arrangements of the School and there is good reason to believe that they are in a satisfactory state'. (This precise form of words suggests that someone might have thought otherwise . . . and, as was proved a few years later, he would have been absolutely right.) The water used for drinking was analysed and pronounced to be of 'excellent quality' but whether this came from their own well or from one of the newly established water companies is not stated.

Throughout these years there was constant praise for Miss Quinan and the zealous and conscientious manner in which she carried out her arduous duties. It is clear that her responsibilities were continually growing and perhaps she did not delegate the actual work sufficiently, as it became a strain which undermined her health. Certainly her treatment of some girls was extremely dictatorial at times, as one Old Girl recalled in 1940 (Edith Boyle, née Russell):

'During the summer exam. in 1882, we were doing geography which was one of my good subjects and I answered all the questions very quickly. Miss Quinan, who was passing through the room, saw me "doing nothing" and came to see about it. I said I had finished my paper, she said it was absurd, and tore my paper into four pieces. More foolscap was handed to me and I was told to answer the questions properly. Of course I could only put down the same answers, and I had 90 out of 100 marks! I don't think any mistress or head would dare to do such a thing nowadays.'

A summary of the numbers and categories of pupils in 1879 shows that out of 79 fathers there were by then 15 Chief Engineers and 12 Paymasters. Captains and Commanders accounted for another 27 girls, the remaining 25 being spread over Lieutenants mainly. Apart from one Vice-Admiral, the rest comprise 4 gallant grandfathers each paying the higher scale of £50 a year.

The financial problems are obvious as one sees that 39 of these girls are 'Elected at £12 a year', another 4 are Nominees of the Royal Patriotic Fund at £10 a year (the condition of their grant of £5000 which helped to pay for St. Margaret's), then there are 19 Nominated by the Committee at £25 a year and finally only 22 who are paying the £50 which could have shown some small margin over actual costs. It is at once clear what very great value for money the School was offering to most of the parents.

In the same Report there is reference to the Queen Adelaide Fund which was making annual grants to help the payment of fees for 3 pupils; this was of great assistance to parents but the School itself derived no pecuniary advantage from the grants. These mundane details are recorded simply as another reminder of how slender was the whole financial basis despite the high distinction of the School's patronage. By its nature it tended to have little contact with those wealthy businessmen some of whom, in that relatively tax-free age, were generous in their charitable disbursements.

A sign of further advancement in teaching methods was the expenditure of £150 on the provision of individual rooms for piano teaching and practice: it appears that the description in *The Beth Book* of the 12 pianos being used at the same time in one room was all too true! This came about as the result of an examination held the previous year by 'eminent and competent professors' and one must commend the decision to have them in and to give effect to their recommendations which also included the engagement of an additional music teacher.

The Annual Examination of the School in the summer of 1879, under the Cambridge University Syndicate conditions, enabled the examiner to report that 'The standard in the Upper Classes, taking one subject with another (perhaps some qualification here?), is highly satisfactory, and the others promising; the tone of the School, as far as I can judge, is excellent'. By this time the Girls' Public Day School Trust, with its excellent High Schools, had been in existence for nearly ten years. As will be seen, Head Mistresses were evolving their own professional standards and it would appear that, according to the Cambridge examiner, the Rev. T. Stephens, M.A., the R.N. Female School was not found wanting.

CHAPTER III

TOWARDS HIGHER STANDARDS

THE start of its fifth decade found St. Margaret's thriving but in a period which made their financial problems no easier because of the prevailing commercial depression. The generation of original subscribers was passing away still more swiftly and it was not being wholly replaced. In one year there was a disconcerting deficit to be met out of reserves and the need for the utmost economy was pressing. Yet at the same time the reputation of the School had never stood higher.

There were remarkable testimonies from various sources, to the good work being done, and heartening evidence of the great extent to which it was valued by both parents and the girls themselves. One parent of a girl for whom the full £50 rate had been paid wrote: 'On return of my daughter from the School, where she has been for several years. . . . I beg you will be good enough to tender to the Committee my sincere thanks for the advantages she has received, and the care that has been uniformly bestowed upon her by the Lady Governess. I am particularly pleased by her manner and appearance, which prove that strict discipline has been tempered by kindness which has led her to have a strong affection for the School and its associations'.

A mother who had three daughters there wrote that she had always felt 'greatly pleased with all the arrangements and very grateful for the kind attention my daughters have invariably met with'. Two of her young ladies showed their appreciation by becoming Life Subscribers. Similar tributes came from some who had been there on the £12 basis, one saying that she intended to become a subscriber after she had left.

There may have been some who shook the dust of St. Margaret's off their feet in much the same manner as did Becky Sharp, of *Vanity Fair* when she left Miss Pinkerton's academy for young ladies, but there seems to be no record of them. Even 'Beth' after she had gone on to a form of Finishing School, looked back upon 'the nicer tone among the Royal Service girls'. In future years there were to be many more who remembered gratefully the benefits and the happiness of their school days, while not forgetting the often irksome degree of discipline.

The death of Miss Clifton in 1882 at the age of 89 was appropriately recorded in the Annual Report and reveals that, born so far back as 1793 – not long after the French Revolution – she must have been 47 when she was appointed Lady Governess. The sheer effort and the achievement of starting up the School from nothing and the move to the far more elaborate establishment at St. Margaret's would have been considerable when she was in her prime, but she continued to run it until 1870 when she would have been 77 years of age – undoubtedly a most remarkable lady. Referring once more to *The Book of Beth,* it is clear from one of Miss Bey's sharp retorts to Beth at the initial interview, that she was considered the Head-Mistress which suggests that Miss Clifton would, at least, have been free of much of the day-to-day detail which must have been associated with the position. One of the qualities which endeared her to so many was, quite possibly, a capacity in later years to stand back a little and exercise her wisdom in an advisory capacity.

In May of the previous year the School had suffered a very serious outbreak of scarlet fever which was, rightly, dreaded in those days. In the words of the Committee it was 'a great cause of thankfulness to Almighty God' that none of the *thirteen* cases that occurred terminated fatally, and very great credit was due to Dr. Fenn and Miss Quinan that the essential extra nursing, the isolation and the subsequent disinfection was carried through efficiently. The 'untiring and self-denying energy' shown by the latter must have taken its toll and led to her early retirement. It is remarkable that the majority of parents, when informed of the outbreak, elected to leave their daughters at the School rather than have them home – as was offered – undoubtedly they had faith in the organization (if not, perhaps, a full realisation of the frightening rapidity with which that infection could sometimes strike down and kill the healthiest child).

This, however, was by no means the end of the troubles for that year of 1882. At the suggestion of Dr. Fenn, a sanitary inspection was ordered, not wholly logically one might think to-day, as the infection was not water-borne, as for example is typhoid, a recurrent anxiety in those days, but the doctor's instinct was sound. The sanitary arrangements of the fine house built by the Earl of Kilmorey, despite the comparatively recent reports to the contrary, proved to be shockingly defective. When it was built that most important of Victorian domestic inventions was not in use – the 'trapped' outlet of the water closet: the simple U-shaped pipe which maintains a permanent water seal to prevent the sewer gases entering the house.

Clearly the vital importance to health of this refinement was not generally realised. It doubtless seemed to many just a new gadget, perhaps to be used if you built a new house, but by no means essential. Such a provision was not, in the 1880s, a legal requirement; after his inspection the Sanitary Authority merely 'recommended' it but the Committee faced the problem resolutely. During a lengthened summer vacation, all the drains and closets were trapped and ventilated and other alterations made 'after the most approved methods'. The cost of all this including the necessary disinfecting and re-decoration was £700; it must have been a severe blow financially and an appeal was made to all subscribers and to Naval Officers generally. They rallied well and just over £1000 came in. The extra sum was extremely useful because the Isleworth Local Board chose that moment to demand £150 from the School for making up the roads bounding their property, preparatory to the Parish taking them over, and also for repairing the river bank. The final episode in sanitary matters came in 1891 when, to meet Thames Conservancy requirements, the School drains were diverted to the local sewage system instead of flowing direct (and untreated) into the river, as formerly.

No apology is offered for this digression into a somewhat unsavoury subject; it was very much a part of Victorian life and to bring the drainage system up to date was the duty of anyone responsible for any large dwelling. The RNS was in no way alone in the crisis it faced, because Uppingham School had been obliged, for the same reason, to remove itself – boys and masters – to a terrace of empty boarding houses in North Wales for an entire term. Miss Quinan and her staff deserved warm congratulations for overcoming the problems involved without more serious disturbance to the work of St. Margaret's.

In the following year came, very understandably, the introduction of what we all knew later as Health Certificates and it was hoped that this precautionary measure would meet with the full co-operation of parents. It could well have been another pioneering effort and one can imagine the reactions of some tough naval fathers whose children had never known a day's illness . . . however it was undoubtedly a sound move.

The surprise of that year – 1883 – was the resignation of Miss Quinan, the Lady Governess, who had obviously borne an exceptional burden of work and additional responsibility in her last years. The Committee gratefully recorded that the character and standard of the School had been greatly raised under her regime and her departure was regretted exceedingly. She had accomplished an immense amount to bring it up to date, the greater number of visits by outside examiners, the additional scholarships and the regular prize-giving all point to this. It must have been very hard for her not to be able to enjoy the further advances which were to be made from the ground which she had gained.

No fewer than 40 candidates applied for her position, still designated as Lady Governess until 1888, when it became that of Lady Principal. This impressive number is some indication of the standing of St. Margaret's and the obvious keenness of the growing number of qualified teachers who wanted this important job.

Miss Jemima Leys, headmistress at Farnworth, Lancs, was chosen, at the age of only 32, and it is particularly interesting that she should have been a former pupil, one who was, in fact, Head Girl in the late 1860s. Thus she had come under the influence of the famous Miss Clifton whom she greatly admired and it is said that – subject to the changing times – she modelled herself on her loved predecessor and retained most of her rules and practices.

Although the customary bouquet to the Lady Governess did not come into the next year's Report, two years later it was stated emphatically that the able Lady Governess had now been in her responsible position for two years and the Committee took the opportunity to record their high opinion of her ability and fitness for her very arduous duties.

Miss Leys was a rather austere character and, on the surface, not very approachable. She used to send for juniors from time to time to say their prayers at her knee. One of them, later Mrs. Holbrook, was once thus summoned and related that she got safely through the Lord's Prayer but then panicked and started off on a long list of 'God bless Mummie, God bless Daddy, God bless sisters, uncles, aunts, etc., until she felt the knees at which she knelt begin to quiver, and a rather tight-voiced Miss Leys said 'I think you might leave God to think of all the rest, you may go to bed'.

Some of her punishments could seem little short of cruel though doubtless not at all exceptional in her day. After prayers each morning mistresses had to report any misbehaviour and a culprit was likely to be told by the Head-mistress, 'You must be unwell to have been so naughty – Mrs. Shales, will you please give her a dose of Gregory Powder'. If the crime was deemed very serious it was 'a dose of Pink Gregory Powder'. The stuff was a peculiarly savage aperient, in which Victorians placed much reliance but it is difficult to see what help it would or could have given to a child probably unhappy or frustrated by the school routines.

Two other forms of admonishment were to enforce the wearing fore and aft of a large placard reading SILENCE for the rest of the day when a girl had been convicted of talking persistently during the many 'silence' periods; it effectively sent her to Coventry. For anyone whose boots or shoes were found lying about the Boot Room floor, instead of being in the appropriate Pigeon Holes, the offending foot-wear was worn strung round her neck for the rest of the day. Boots were the more usual wear, in those days, and the discomfort of one or two pairs dangling on their long laces (which cut into the neck of the victim) can be easily imagined. Not only in 'The Mikado' were punishments made to fit the crime.

In writing to their parents on Sundays the girls would often have to include at the end some such phrase as: 'Miss Leys wishes me to say that I am a good child'. Sometimes adding, 'but she is shocked at my spelling'. Equally she might 'wish me to say that I am lazy and could do better' . . . (of how many girls and boys has this been said and yet how large a proportion of them have buckled to and worked well directly they come under the inspiration of the right teacher!).

How far the marked advance in scholastic standards was due to the new Lady Governess one cannot say but the appointment of Miss Leys coincided with interesting and valuable changes. In 1884 definite standards were set for the award of prizes in the usual school subjects, 75% of possible marks for a First Class and 60% for a Second. A prize for Darning was a sound idea – that thankless task so vital, then, in any household run economically, and in days when wool and flannel predominated. Nylon underwear was still about 60 years ahead and long before central heating was general you needed something warm 'next the skin'. Many an 'N.O.'s wife' must have been thankful for a daughter who could turn to upon the family darning if need be! Embroidery was another prize subject.

It was also realised that the Entrance Exam questions had remained unaltered for 12 years and they were thoroughly revised being made more difficult, for the most part, to bring them into conformity with the School's curriculum. Pleasant period questions like naming 'the British possessions in North America and Africa' mingled with the mathematical horrors of finding 'the number of square poles in 3758462 square inches'.

A particularly significant item in 1885 was that 7 girls were entered for the Oxford Local Examination, held at Burlington House, a Free Church girls' school at Isleworth. Of these 6 passed, 3 with honours, receiving one guinea each as a prize. Of 913 candidates from all over England, only 38 girls passed well enough among the Juniors to be placed in the second division and of these *three* were Royal Naval pupils. It was quite a triumph and furnished impressive proof that whatever else might be said of the School it was succeeding in its primary purpose.

The earlier efforts to improve the music teaching were also bringing good results. All new girls were given tuition, presumably in piano playing, free for their first term. Thereafter, if they continued, 7 shillings per term was paid if they were taught by one of the 'Resident Music Governesses' or 10 shillings if by a visiting Master; presumably the more promising girls were given the chance of male instruction. (These fees were very modest; at Cheltenham piano was £2 per term minimum.) It was found to be worthwhile for the distinguished organist and choirmaster of the Chapel Royal, Windsor, Dr. Walter Parrat, to examine them in music more than once and he appears to have reported favourably. Shortly after his first visit the School received from Mrs. C. R. Edgerton the gift of a 'Collard Grand Pianoforte in good condition' which would have done much to add to the effect and sense of occasion at the School concerts, as well as being a real encouragement for the more gifted pianists among the pupils.

Another advance towards a more modern organization at this time was the decision to make divisions into an Upper and Lower School, with the proviso that all pupils at 16 years of age must pass into the Upper School. If they were not equal to this, they had to be removed from St. Margaret's. This was strictly adhered to, the Committee observing that any relaxation of the rules, instead of being an advantage to 'the rejected young ladies, would rather have been a drawback, besides being an injury to those remaining'. Hard it must have seemed for those who failed, but there were very few of them and the principle was sound.

Meanwhile the School doubtless benefited from the good work of the Association of Headmistresses. The famous Frances Mary Buss and Dorothea Beale had arranged their first meeting in London in 1874 by which time the movement for girls' education was well under way. The nine pioneers attending represented London schools for the most part except for Miss Beale, who was, of course, Cheltenham, but their numbers soon grew and from 1877 annual conferences were held. Remembering that in the 1870s railway travel was something of an adventure especially for unaccompanied ladies, it showed enthusiasm to be able to hold these meetings – and in various parts of the country. They would have been expected to pay their own expenses – unlike most delegates to conferences nowadays – and they found the experience immensely worthwhile as those from schools of fewer than one hundred had opportunity to learn from the Heads of much larger establishments. In 1896 Alice Morison, Headmistress of Truro High School, signed a conference register below a famous name so that it read:

Dorothea Beale, Cheltenham	999 pupils
Alice R. Morison, Truro	99 pupils

The very large number of the former surprises one but it comes from an impeccable authority, the official centenary publication of the Association of Headmistresses, *Reluctant Revolutionaries,* by Nonita Glenday and Mary Price, from which these details are drawn.

These fine women, many of them neatly bonnetted, appear to us in the early photographs as so many grandmothers, but many of them were still only in their twenties when they took on their responsibilities. They could possess no paper qualifications before 1880 when London first admitted women to degrees, to be followed soon by Trinity College, Dublin. Oxford, as is well known, held out against giving degrees to women until 1921, though women's colleges had existed there since the 1880s. The early headmistresses were usually strong in their foreign languages, probably through some residence abroad, and where they had some Latin and Greek it was often due to the help of father or an elder brother. They were well read and knew their Bibles thoroughly so that their religious teaching was never in doubt.

Though they had formerly led sheltered lives their new appointments would have plunged them into unfamiliar dealings with builders, tradesmen and suppliers of various kinds – long before those capable ex-officers of Army and Navy had been drawn into school business as Bursars. Like St. Margaret's, most girls' schools were short of money and wishing to keep their fees low, so that the utmost economy was essential in their management. The exacting task of the headmistress was not made easier by having to run her school in premises which had not been designed for the purpose and were often far from ideal. It was all a very long way from the luxurious custom-built 'Comprehensive' of to-day and reflects the greater credit upon those pioneers.

By comparison with the present, they had one great advantage: people did then expect to obey those in authority over them whether they were children in relation to parents, or teachers, or again junior staff in relation to their seniors. Thus a Head possessed considerable power over her staff. To take a couple of odd examples: in one school junior teachers were told very firmly by their headmistress that she objected to their reading of *Jane Eyre,* it was unsuitable for them until they were twenty-five years old! In the 1880s the bicycle and its associated clothes were seen as a danger point for respectability and one of the staff at Swansea High School was dismissed outright for cycling through a suburban street clad in her bloomers – such was the absolute power of the headmistress.

In 1887 the Association was honoured to receive an invitation from Dr. Edward Thring to hold their annual conference at Uppingham School. The occasion proved a great success – he set out to treat them royally – and found them a very remarkable set of able and interesting women. Addressing them he said: 'You are fresh and enthusiastic and comparatively untrammelled whilst we are weighed down by tradition, cast like iron in the rigid moulds of the past . . . the hope of teaching lies in you'. Words of great encouragement for the visitors which must have helped to consolidate the growing sense of professionalism amongst them.

So, it can be seen from these threads that girls' schools for the middle classes were becoming firmly established and the 'Royal Naval', once almost alone, now had many others beside it with whom experience could be compared, and from whom a wider choice of teachers could be obtained when needed.

It is interesting now to see, in some detail, just how the School appeared from a girl's standpoint. One Old Girl of 1880 – 1886 wrote:

'Never shall I forget the appalling cold of St. Margaret's from October until the summer came, for there was no artificial heat. During the winter months we tramped round and round the gravel paths in the garden three or four times a day, always getting colder and colder. I think one thing which made me so cold was the introduction of 'cocoa' for breakfast. I simply could not drink 'sweet cocoa', and very much missed my unsweetened cups of hot tea.

'In those days we were never allowed to speak on the stairs or in the bed-rooms, and I remember being reported for nudging Bessie Eckford to call her attention to a beautiful sunset, as we came downstairs!'

Here is another, a fascinating account of life at St. Margaret's about 1890 written by a remarkable lady, Miss Ruth Chignell, in 1940, when she must have been some sixty years of age:

'When I went to the School at the age of ten . . . , there were many things in its routine which a modern girl would not tolerate for a week – but before I begin to describe them, I must say emphatically that I owe a debt of gratitude to the School nevertheless.

'We received an exceedingly good education . . . with mental and moral training which made us fit to take responsible positions in after-life, and to do our work with a high sense of duty. Perhaps the easiest way is to describe an average school day in winter, so that present girls can compare it with their own. I began School life as the youngest child in the lowest form and I ended it as Head Girl. I was a 'good' child at first, a 'naughty' one in the middle of the School and something of a prig at the end . . . and the regime did not change much during my eight years there.

'At 6.15 a maid clattered along the corridor, ringing the bell and we had to get up at once. If we did not the Bedroom Monitress came and pulled the bedclothes from the bed. Every girl had a small footbath under her washstand, and was supposed to take a bath in it, fortunately no steps were taken to see that she did so, because the water was cold. Not until a year or so before I left did maids come in and pour 'hot' water into our basins . . . and the water was often tepid. [Even so, the labour for the poor maids, including removing all the 'slops' must have been formidable!]

'At seven another bell rang and we had to pull back our curtains at once and kneel down and say our prayers, at which time the mistress in charge dashed in to see if we were dressed. We were given ten minutes for prayers and were allowed to read 'Bible, Prayer Book and one religious manual'. A Rule was that 'every pupil must go to the bathroom in slippers and dressing gown and on returning go at once into bed' (the language always caused me to give a mental chuckle and I visualised myself *going into* a tunnel). "No talking is allowed in the bedrooms, bedroom passages, or on the staircases, before breakfast, after the gas is out, or in the interval in the evening before the second prayer bell".

'At 7.15 we had the first lesson of the day. At 7.45 assembly and prayers in the hall, followed by breakfast in the basement dining rooms. No talking was allowed at any meal except in the small dining room where Miss Leys took one end of the table . . . and to which only the girls who had the highest places in the top form were admitted. Breakfast consisted of cocoa and bread and butter – never anything else. Both were good, and no doubt we fared well enough, for we might have an unlimited supply – but it was very dull, especially for the poor things who did not like cocoa. The Mistresses had something in the way of bacon, sausage, or egg, but carefully apportioned to their numbers. [Such a distinction, providing so much less protein for growing children, may seem incredible to-day but it was not unusual at the time.]

'Directly after breakfast we had to dash upstairs, make our beds, and leave everything scrupulously tidy. The maids had done the washstands while we were at breakfast, so no one could blame anyone else for disorderliness, and bad marks were given by the Mistress to any girl whose shoes were found under her bed instead of in her shoe box, or whose hair brush was not in its bag. These bad marks were read out in the hall after evening prayers, and were considered a disgrace to the class to which the victim belonged.

'By 8.25 we had to be out in the garden, duly clad in winter clothing, and wearing gloves, hat and goloshes. Bad marks again if the Mistress on duty found us with gloves in pockets instead of on hands. At 8.55 the big bell was rung, and we had to dash in, put all our outdoor garments in their proper places, collect our books and pencil boxes from classrooms, and take our places in the big schoolroom for the Scripture lesson. This Miss Leys always took herself, with all the classes together except the two lowest, who were included on Saturdays only when the two highest were not included.

'It was worth while being at the School for those Scripture lessons alone, for our knowledge of the Bible and Prayer Book was far beyond that possessed by other people whom I came across later in life and high moral standards of duty grew with our knowledge. Every girl had to learn two verses from some chapter of the Bible every day, and to repeat them aloud perfectly at the beginning of the lesson, finally repeating the whole chapter. I fancy that modern children would be surprised to be made to learn all the names of the books of the Bible in proper order, with the number of the chapters in each, Genesis 50, Exodus 40, Leviticus 27, and so on; but that was the first thing that every new girl had to learn, even if she was only ten, and I for one liked saying the strange names aloud.

'After the Scripture lesson we scattered to our own classrooms. There was a short break of fifteen minutes, in which the ceremony of goloshes and gloves had to be gone through again, for we were turned out in all weathers, unless there was a positive downpour, when we joyfully paced the hall and passages instead of going out. Some girls had "special" milk during the interval, and bread and butter was provided for anyone who wanted it; but in my day it was considered mollycoddle to have either, and very few girls went to the little luncheon room.

'Lessons continued till 12.35, and once again we went to the garden. Dinner was at 1.15 [no mention of the food but supposedly it was a good substantial meal]. Directly after dinner we had to go for a dreary walk, two by two, with a teacher at the back of each party . . . we had to talk French[1] all day until after evening prayers, so the chatter was not what it might have been . . . the two girls who walked with the Mistress were allowed to speak English to her, so she never lacked for a couple of eager companions.

'Wednesday was the best afternoon of the week as we were allowed longer time for the walk and could get as far as Richmond Park or Kew Gardens, crossing the river by ferry as the two great bridges were not there then. Afternoon lessons began at 3 p.m. and went on till 5.30 when we had to dash upstairs, change our frocks, and be down again for tea at 5.45.

'Tea consisted again of nothing but tea and bread and butter but at this meal we were allowed to bring out of the "goody cupboard" any cakes, biscuits or jam we had had sent from home.

'After tea the whole evening was given up to preparation for the next day's lessons. We were not allowed to call it prep. as all abbreviations were considered unladylike in those days. Preparation was a very solemn affair. No word was spoken, no desk might be opened, no girl might leave her seat, all for fear of disturbing those around her. . . . All books, pens, rulers, had to be taken out of the desk before 6.15 and put on the floor beside us, so that the banging of a desk could at no time disturb the silence of the room. It was a good scheme for we really did work, and had no temptation to waste our time.

'Then came evening assembly and prayers at 8 and after that, the most blessed half hour of the day, when we might talk English and walk freely in the passages or classrooms with our friends. Supper of bread and water was provided but attendance in the dining room was optional and many preferred to spend the precious time with their friends.

'I am afraid we did not wash very enthusiastically, for the water in our jugs was only tepid – but we kept a sharp ear on each other to make sure that every girl *did* wash and clean her teeth! Our turn for a bath in the bathroom . . . came only once a week [very usual in Victorian times], as there were only five baths in the whole school.

'And that was our programme day by day throughout the term, except that on Wednesday evening we had dancing lessons by an unattractive little lady with marvellously small feet, clad in cloth boots with no heels. She could not keep any sort of discipline, so Miss Fitch played the piano and kept us in order with the back of her head. . . .

'Sunday was a pleasant day to us, making such a contrast to the others, but I doubt whether modern girls would think it so. We got up at 7 instead of 6.15, but there was never an early service, partly for the convenience of the Chaplain, who came from London, but mainly for the convenience of the maids, who got very little free time, and counted on Sunday as their best day. Before morning

[1](in which 'Passez-moi the butter, or dites-moi what you said' etc. was about the normal level of conversation).

service in the Chapel, we had Prayer Book and Catechism lessons. Every girl had to learn the Catechism perfectly, questions as well as answers, from beginning to end, and then go on to the other parts of the Prayer Book.

'I think the Service in the Chapel was rather dull. The choir sat in the two front seats, with their backs to the rest of the School, and did not give a very good lead in the singing to those behind them. . . .

'A few visitors from the outer world usually attended our Chapel, and for that strange reason our Mistresses were all required to wear bonnets on Sunday to distinguish them from the elder girls. How some of them hated it! When I myself became a Mistress at the School, there was no such thing as a bonnet to be found in any milliner's shop; but Miss Leys was still adamant, so Miss McKie made me one, of black lace over pink satin, with black velvet strings. It sounds awful but I assure you that it was rather becoming and I rather fancied myself in it. . . .

'Dinner was always cold on Sunday, to let the maids get out as early as possible; but the sweet was always a tart of some sort, and we liked that and enjoyed the Sunday dinner.

'After dinner we walked in the garden until 3, then came in to learn the Collect, Epistle and Gospel for the day, or parts of them if we were still young. The top form had special work to do for Miss Leys, being supposed to know the Collects, etc., by the time they reached that form. Hers was a delightful lesson, most carefully prepared by herself, with a series of questions previously set us, for which we had to search the Scriptures to find the answer. The lessons followed at once after the preparation, and then tea. No special provision for tea, but on rare occasions we found slabs of rich brown cake on the table. No one might go to the goody cupboard on Sunday, as Mrs. Shales (the House-keeper who kept the key) must not be delayed that day.

'Evening Service followed directly after tea, and then the happy half hour, again with one's friends, before going to bed, with no assembly on Sunday night. Does it sound a dull day to a modern girl? Well, I know that most of the girls of my day enjoyed Sunday, and looked forward to it week by week.

'We played hockey in the winter and tennis in the summer, clad in long skirts with tight belts, and blouses with tight sleeves and high stiff collars. And we played croquet with wide hoops almost capable of letting through two balls at once . . . but in these matters we were not peculiar, for all young women of the time had to do the same. Ours was one of the first of the girls' public schools to introduce Swedish Drill. Miss Leys told me that Madame Bergmann Osterberg went to the School to give the first few lessons herself, being only a beginner in England and very glad of the patronage of a good school. We had relays of Osterberg Mistresses to take drill (not then known as gym.) all the time I was at School, but they carefully wore long skirts over their tunics, as did we all, at all times when we were not actually in the drill house. I can remember a man coming to take a photograph of our class at work for publication in some magazine, and the Mistress dashing into the corner to put her skirt on before she would have it taken!

'We did not enjoy the drill classes; they were not as merry as gym. is now. But I can still climb a rope . . . and I am a most healthy woman . . . and what more can one want?'

One realizes from this account, by an obviously responsible and reliable witness, that aspects of the School routine in 1890 could have been seen as unnecessarily draconian and repressive yet there is no suggestion that many girls were miserable under it. On the contrary, St. Margaret's appears to have been essentially a 'happy ship'. Like many of her contemporaries, the writer looks back with appreciation upon her time there and all that it did for her, and she took the opportunity to return later as a teacher. The general conditions seem to have been similar to those of other schools, and the standards of work above average.

To fill in a few more details of that fifth decade one must, of course, mention that the School dutifully added to the thousands of tributes sent to Queen Victoria, their Royal Patron, on the occasion of her Jubilee in 1887, though there is no record of their enjoying any special holiday or treat to celebrate the day. The Duchess of Albany did, however, distribute the prizes that year; otherwise there is suggestion of a certain financial stringency and Miss Leys is again commended for 'economical management of the domestic arrangements' – more luxurious breakfasts were obviously still some years ahead!

Examination results continued well with twelve out of fourteen candidates passing their Oxford Local which seems fair enough out of only about 77 pupils in all, many of them under twelve years of age. It appears too, that the standard of music must have been relatively high in that so distinguished a man as Dr. Walter Parrat (soon to be knighted) of Windsor should continue to examine them each year, reporting well upon the progress of their piano work and singing.

Though it is not our business, after all these years, one cannot help wondering what exactly was the trouble at that time which caused the School 'with much regret to request, as an example, the withdrawal of two of the elder pupils for misconduct, which if unchecked would have seriously influenced the tone and discipline of the whole school'. The wording suggests some form of insubordination: it is hard to believe that the misconduct could have approached anything comparable to the appalling behaviour one hears of to-day in some establishments, but the treatment meted out must have ensured that there was no recurrence.

In 1889, in order to offer still better value in the hope of attracting more pupils it was decided to include music and deportment, without extra charge, in the ordinary curriculum. 'Callisthenics' were also part of it, giving opportunity 'for a healthy recreation'. The strange fact is that neither in the Annual Report or Accounts of those years does one find any reference to Sports yet Miss Chignell mentions croquet, tennis and hockey specifically in 1890 and it seems unlikely that they could have been started only in that year. Here for once, the Committee seem to have 'missed a trick' in their continual though discreet mention of the School's advantages. The laying out of playing fields and the equipment must all have involved extra expense but it is not shown in the expenditure for any year and had some sporting benefactor donated it he would surely have been publicly thanked, one imagines. Be that as it may, the RNS was obviously up to date in this matter as will be seen from the records of matches played against other schools in the New Century.

The following year brought up their own Jubilee and in presenting the Fiftieth Report of the 'Proceedings of The Royal Naval Female School' the Committee were 'deeply sensible of the Divine support which has attended the efforts of all who are concerned in carrying on the work of the Institution, and they humbly rely upon the blessing of Almighty God for a continued course of usefulness'. They looked back over half a century of faith, hope and extremely hard work which had undoubtedly brought their own reward. Their successors can feel that the humble reliance expressed on that occasion in 1890 was not unfulfilled.

CHAPTER IV

INTO THE NEW CENTURY

AT the start of our new period there came a domestic event which, though small in itself, can perhaps be seen as having genuine significance. It was decided that as the Institute was essentially for the benefit of young ladies, 'Ladies might be admitted to the Board of Management as questions will sometimes arise in which their advice may be of great advantage'! This was decided by a majority but was evidently not a unanimous vote; initially just two women braved the formerly all-male gathering of thirty. It appears extraordinary that for the first fifty years there should have been no feminine voice in the top management of a girls' school but one has to remember that in Victorian times the committee woman was distinctly a *rara avis,* save for organizations such as the Head-mistresses' Association which were initiated by, and for, women. Dr. Barnardo's Homes, for all their concern for child life, had no woman on their committee until 1938. So, there was another step forward for the RNS.

A further, and quite major, improvement was the change of name which may well have been due to one of those ladies on the Committee. Realising that the original name with its somewhat dreary word 'female' did not indicate specifically that it was a place for *children* the name was changed to the *Royal School for the Daughters of Officers of the Royal Navy & Royal Marines.* Not so concise as the present form perhaps, but it had a fine ring to it and described its purpose precisely. At the same time Miss Leys was accorded the title of 'Lady Principal' which must have been more in conformity with general practice than the somewhat archaic term 'Governess' by which she and her predecessors had been designated.

The President of the School was now Admiral H.R.H. the Duke of Edinburgh, one of Queen Victoria's sons. He presided over a Jubilee Dinner held in the, then comparatively new, Hotel Metropole in Northumberland Avenue where he successfully launched a special appeal which raised just over £1000 and included useful donations from several City Livery Companies such as the Goldsmiths, Mercers, Grocers and Vintners. This was extremely valuable as the Committee continually had difficulty in balancing costs against receipts and any substantial additional items had to come from some extraneous source. Over the years it can be said, in all sincerity, that their labours furnished an amazing example of the oft-quoted saying that 'God helps those who help themselves' and they would continually have been admirable recipients for that form of charity favoured by Victorians, the 'challenge grant', i.e. if *you* can raise a given sum the prospective donor will double it.

The core of their financial problem at this stage was that, not only were they not absolutely full up – 73 pupils when they could accommodate up to 82 – but 37 were on the minimum £12 a year basis and only 18 at the full £50 rate. Another 9 at £50 would have made just all the difference and 'the oldest girls' boarding school' could fairly claim to be offering exceptional value for money. A wise move in 1899 was to agree to admit the daughters of civilians at the full terms

50

and a year later those of officers in the Royal Indian Marine. The Colonial Marine Services were, at that time, normally officered by men of the R.N. Reserve. It was reasonably pointed out in one Report that if one-twentieth of the officers in the Navy List would give a small annual contribution to the funds of the School they would then be equal to the demands upon them. Although it had been unavoidable to dip into the invested funds occasionally, they still stood at £27,000 (yielding barely 3 %) plus a further substantial sum of which the interest provided the income for the various scholarships.

Curiously enough the first actual reference to games facilities does not feature until 1898 when the Oxford Examination Delegacy examiner the Rev. W. H. Fairbrother of Lincoln College stated in his report 'A word ought to be added as to the exceptional advantages the School enjoys in buildings and in opportunities for out-door exercise. Nothing could be better than the accommodation in these respects'. There is also mention, a year later, of the provision of hard tennis courts, which were surely a comparatively modern innovation and it seems remarkable that not more was made of this development in the Annual Reports of a practically all-male committee. However the important point is that those young girls then had something pleasanter and more stimulating for their recreation time than those tedious walks about the grounds or the streets.

Royalty continued to demonstrate that its patronage was no mere formality. For the marriage of Princess May (future Queen Mary) to the Duke of York (future George V) in July 1893, Queen Victoria 'was graciously pleased to command a stand to be erected in the garden of Buckingham Palace for the use of pupils and teachers to view the Royal Procession'. The School was very much indebted to Admiral the Hon. Sir Francis Edgerton for his kind offices in this matter. We should mention that the bride, then Duchess of York, having survived the intense fatigue of a very hot wedding day, ending with a particularly dusty drive from the railway station to York Cottage, Sandringham, was so good as to come – a year or so later – to visit the School with her mother, the Duchess of Teck. Readers with any personal knowledge of the late, and much admired, Queen Mary, will know that her eye for domestic detail was penetrating and her visits were never perfunctory. It was a triumph for Miss Leys and her entire staff, both teaching and domestic, that the distinguished visitors 'expressed themselves greatly pleased with all they saw'.

While there appears to have been no special arrangement for the School to attend that tremendous affair of the Diamond Jubilee procession in London they had, as will be seen later a memorable time at the Coronation of King George and Queen Mary in 1911. With the death of Queen Victoria came the severing of the particular royal link which had extended throughout the entire existence of the School but it was a great pleasure for them to be assured that King Edward would continue the patronage he had accepted throughout most of his years as Prince of Wales. Only the postponement of his Coronation, due to his illness in June 1902, prevented the School from being able to enjoy the seats which had been reserved for them near the Palace. The ceremony did not, of course, take place until the school holiday month of August.

Turning to purely St. Margaret's matters again, by the end of the century the finances were in slightly better shape, gaining from the bold decision to put up the full fee rate from £50 to £60 per annum. At this level they were well below their most distinguished competitor Cheltenham – if one may so describe that great school. At the same time exam results were good: the 15 girls sent in for the Oxford Local and the 14 for the College of Preceptors all passed in 1901 – and this from a total of only 76 pupils in the whole School. They had to wait another four years before the next development which was to put St. Margaret's into the position of being continually full up with a waiting list.

It appears that the location of the School beside the sometimes damp and misty bank of the Thames had come in for some unfavourable comment because the Committee went to the trouble of obtaining a report from the local Medical Officer of Health. He was able to assure them that the death rate of St. Margaret's – the suburb of that name, not the School! – was 12–14 per 1000 of population which was well below the national average, that the soil was gravel and the water supply both good and abundant. The drainage of the School House was good and over 30 years the percentage of infectious cases had proved remarkably small. It was 'fair enough' so far as it went, though one would naturally expect the death rate of a well-to-do residential area in those days to be below the national average. The report did not deal with the exceptional cold which was associated with the house, especially before central heating had been installed, but in that respect it was possibly little worse than many other similar buildings.

In the same year as that of the medical officer's inspection there were reported most generous contributions to the School by benefactors who appear anonymous: one of them chartered an entire Thames steamboat to take all the School on a river trip upon the day when they should have been going to the Coronation in June, something which would obviously come as a great treat for them. Then there was 'a kind friend of the Institute' who nobly footed the bill of £527 for the provision of new lavatories and bathrooms and general re-decoration.

In 1904 came news, doubtless much regretted at the time, which none the less prepared the way for the next big advance. Miss Leys resigned at the end of July, after 21 years. She would have been no more than in her early fifties but was already suffering the cruel disabilities of rheumatoid-arthritis. The Committee's wish that 'she may long enjoy a peaceful and happy retirement in private life' suggests that she gave up teaching then. Under her management the School had in their words 'gained a reputation for its high moral tone and prominent position . . . which will redound to her credit'. She appears to have been able, very skilfully to effect a large measure of transformation, from the purely Victorian type of school which she took over in 1883, without causing serious upheavals or dissension by the way. It would seem that by 1904 it was already offering all the subjects and means of learning available in other schools and it was well placed to move ahead in the new teaching methods which were to develop so swiftly in the 20th century.

The appointment of Miss Leys' successor marked a new age. She was Miss Helen Stone, B.A. London, who had been Headmistress of the High School for

Girls at Cirencester; she was a complete professional, already experienced as a headmistress and for the first time it had been possible for St. Margaret's to have one possessing a degree. As before there had been a large number of applicants and once again the Committee had chosen wisely. Very early they were able to recognise gratefully the many improvements which Miss Stone soon introduced.

Curiously enough at this stage the Annual Report becomes even terser and less informative than in earlier years but fortunately copies of the excellent School Magazine *The Victory* are available from 1906. The first bound volume of them has a frontispiece photograph of Miss Stone showing a woman of some beauty whose serious expression combines strength and sensitivity.

At once we are plunged happily into the Speech Day of 1905 with bouquets for both Miss Stone, and Lady Curzon-Howe who gives away the prizes. Seventeen prizes and many certificates are given out as well as 14 Good Conduct Badges. A 'very creditable' music programme follows with the Senior Singing Class rendering Smart's immortal anthem 'How Lovely are Thy dwellings' – the inevitable Chopin 'Valse (A major)' – Sinding's 'Rustle of Spring' . . . and not forgetting a French recitation. Then on to The Speech given by Admiral Bowden-Smith who, in the course of his stirring address praises 'gallant Admiral Togo who had won for his country such triumphs in the China Sea'. Specimens of the School's drawing work are on display and the natural history collections made by the girls during their summer holidays. It all has an utterly familiar ring to those with memory of prize days in later years but it must have brightened many young lives at the time.

Other entertainments of the period included a 'Lantern Lecture' on the Navy and it *would* doubtless have been an oil-lit lantern or, at best, a lime-light dependent upon the uncertainties of rubber tubing and a hissing oxygen cylinder; there was no question then of a neat electrically-lit projector and the profusion of colour transparencies which every lecturer can produce today. By 1906 the story of the Navy could just have included the great sensation of the new *Dreadnought* battleship which was launched in 1905. The first all-big-gun battleship to be driven by turbines, she could steam at over twenty knots, as compared with fourteen – the previous maximum for such a class of ship – and she rendered all other battleships obsolete. This, as all naval fathers knew (and probably many of their daughters too!) was the work of the indomitable Admiral Lord Fisher whose many reforms over the previous ten years had achieved so much for the Senior Service.

Still on the lighter side of School life, there was at this time an 'undress performance' of *Julius Caesar*, certainly a move in the right direction, though before long means were found for the girls to enjoy the unfailing pleasures of 'dressing up' for all their plays. Forms I, II and III were responsible for this Shakespearean production and one would love to know what they made of it in those Edwardian days.

Before leaving these pleasures one must pay tribute to a certain Mr. J. A. Mullens, Stockbroker to the Bank of England, who proved himself, over a number of years, to be a most generous and imaginative benefactor. He arranged a series of annual summer outings, usually on some part of the river. One involved a steamer trip down to Greenwich in the course of which some rude boys shouted 'Votes for Women!' and 'Suffragettes' at the boat-load of girls as they passed under one of the London bridges ('which afforded us much amusement' said the account in their magazine) – it was typical of the cockney humour of the day.

The Zoo, and the Japanese Exhibition at Earls Court were other expeditions arranged in different years but one of Mr. Mullens' finest hours must have been his full day's outing to Windsor in 1906. The organization appears to have been well nigh faultless. As Sybil Woolton described it for the magazine: 'On the eventful morning we were all delighted to see a cloudless sky. Rising at an early hour we were able to leave the School by 7.30 and an hour later found us at Molesey (near Hampton Court) after a pleasant journey from Richmond in two electric cars which Mr. Mullens had kindly provided for us. (London United Tramways had reached the area a year or two before.) Then came an anxious wait, for there was no steamer to be seen, but all fears were dissipated when at nine oclock it hove in sight. The river was beautiful . . . as the boat glided along, now between broad meadows with Alderney cows, now past picturesque villas with their smooth green lawns spreading down to the river, while numerous houseboats showed every variety of gay colour and bright flowers. At Chertsey Lock Mr. Mullens and two of his grand-children joined us and then again, to the strains of a gramophone, the boat proceeded on its way. As we approached Windsor, the river, studded with many islands, narrowed considerably and shortly after noon we had our first glimpse of the Castle.' [It is a vivid picture of the pleasures of the river in its pre-1914 heyday.] They went on to have lunch on board then 'in a crocodile of many feet we wended our way to the Castle, the long line of girls in dark blue suits, white blouses and sailor hats with naval hatbands, having a pleasing effect . . .' So on to St. George's Chapel and parts of the Castle. They started for home at 3.30, had tea on board, and were back at Molesey by 8 p.m. where the two special tramcars were awaiting them; so home by 9 p.m. all agreeing that they had spent a very happy day!

The very generous and thoughtful Mullens consolidated his good work by donating a capital sum to be invested and to accumulate for his lifetime, thereafter the interest to be used to pay for future outings. He must have given a great deal of enjoyment to the School. Actually his fund continues to this day, though used for other purposes.

During her first year at St. Margaret's Miss Stone succeeded in getting the most distinguished headmistress in England, Dorothea Beale, to visit them and that in itself must have added to the stature of the School.

After reading with deep conviction from I Thessalonians V. vv. 5–15 Miss Beale had given to the girls a most impressive address based upon those matchless words of St. Paul: 'Ye are all the children of light . . . be sober putting on the breastplate of faith and love . . . be at peace among yourselves . . . see that none render evil for evil with any man; but ever follow that which is good'. Then in her seventies, she died only a year later, and as one of the many obituaries pointed out, among her great achievements had been to transform Cheltenham from a school of 69 pupils in a private house into a college of over 1000 with magnificent buildings and a world-wide reputation. Miss Beale was rightly regarded as the leader of the Renaissance in women's education: she had striven not primarily to make women learned but to fit them for the work of life, however humble or however dignified their vocation. The aims and ideals of St. Margaret's were, in their own way, developing very closely in line with those of the great Educationist who visited them in 1905.

The vocations of the R.N. girls after leaving School now showed much greater variety than in the earlier years and there were fewer references to their taking posts as governesses. Doubtless many of them still did so and made a thorough success of the work but it is refreshing to read, in the early 1900s, that some were taking up Nursing, that Physical Education was growing fast as a profession for women and, of course, a great many of them were getting married.

Almost every issue of *The Victory* had a detailed account of some Old Girl's wedding and there are splendid touches, such as that of a ceremony in Cheshire where not only were the page boys all dressed in 'white men-of-war suits with Jack Tar hats, but the path leading to the church was lined by little girls from the Liverpool Seamen's Orphanage – all of whose fathers had lost their lives at sea'. These children each wore a blue serge sailor dress with a red rose and they strewed roses at the feet of the happy couple as they left the church. The music of the service and the details of the bride's clothes are always given in full; this was no more than the custom of the time but it comes as an interesting surprise and one cannot help wondering what some of the earlier Vice-Patronesses would have thought about such nuptial details being flourished before girls who were still at school. Actually these good ladies are not mentioned after the Report of 1893 and it appears that their visits were then discontinued but they no doubt rendered a useful service before there were ladies on the Committee.

In 1906 the Liberal Party were returned to Parliament with their great majority which was to lead on to vast social changes, one of which was the measure of the Workmen's Compensation Act. Under this the Committee 'thought it imperative to insure the Educational Staff and the servants against accidents .... at a present cost of £5. 15s. a year .... ' which comes to us 70 years later as a sharp reminder of the former vulnerability of the employee in case of accident to him, or her, while at work. This same year brought the School – again through the kindness of an anonymous benefactor – the use of a good new playing field at Marble Hill, near Twickenham. It gave ample space for cricket, which was now played for the first time, and for hockey. A 'hockey group' – curiously of 21 players – posed before a beautiful leafless elm tree two years later shows a very fine gathering of senior girls in smart white blouses, neat high collars (some of them starched?), ties and dark serge skirts well below the knee. All appear terribly constricting but such was the case with most dress in those days; the point is that the girls look keen and some are obviously enjoying themselves.

A scene on the tennis courts in St. Margaret's grounds suggests a slower tempo; the nets droop somewhat in the centre, no side or end netting is visible and the girls' skirts are longer; nevertheless they *are* going at it seriously and they are learning a game which can be of delightful value to them later: private tennis parties were very much part of the social scene before 1914. At risk of over-emphasis one must say again that they were moving well with the times, in this respect, and there is news of plenty of matches played against other schools of which Streatham Hill and Surbiton High Schools are regular fixtures.

Thus, the latter part of the Edwardian era saw the School moving serenely ahead and well up to the general standards of other comparable establishments. Certainly some of the visiting teams must have been greatly impressed by the imposing appearance and situation of the late Earl of Kilmorey's mansion. The girls of Surbiton High School, for example, came from a rabbit warren of two large old houses, albeit well maintained, but joined together by a covered bridge, and situated beside a busy road along which electric trams thundered frequently, to disturb the words of the teachers. (Though presided over by a dragon-headmistress they, too, achieved good results.)

Probably as a result of Miss Stone's regime and her personal reputation the School was now entirely full up and actually in need of more accommodation. Financially they still had not a penny to spare because the proportion of those on reduced fees remained very high. To that extent St. Margaret's was fulfilling its purpose most admirably but the Committee still had to appeal each year for more subscriptions and for more parents prepared to send their daughters at full fees.

In 1908 Mr. Samuel Royson who had acted as Secretary for 54 years, decided to retire and was awarded a pension of £150 p.a. This gave the opportunity for the engagement of a Miss Todd as secretary to work at the School, so it became possible to save the expense of the London office in Sackville Street. With the entry of a lady who was doubtless a trained shorthand-typist, whatever her other qualifications may have been, came the need for a 'typewriter machine' and this was provided by some kind donor. Thereafter the labour of preparing notices and the copies of exam papers must have been considerably eased.

Strangely enough, in the following year, came the first case of appendicitis and one of the girls was successfully operated upon. It was often said that King Edward's operation in 1902 had made that complaint 'fashionable' and possibly this treatment was thereafter administered more frequently than was absolutely necessary but one prefers to regard it as one more of the blessed medical discoveries which helped to save many a young life.

A curious feature which appeared regularly in the Annual Report during these years was a frontispiece photograph of the 'Interior of Hall'. It replaced earlier views of the exterior of St. Margaret's, all rather magnificent in themselves, and giving some idea of the fine extent of the grounds. This picture of the Hall, by contrast suggested nothing but gloom. It was dominated by a broad flight of steps leading up from glass doors to the garden which seem to serve no useful purpose but which must have let in a lot of cold air in winter. They were flanked by enormous twisted baroque style pillars of quite exceptional ugliness but of a sort beloved by many 19th century architects – these gave a vaguely barbaric air to the large room and must have been awe-inspiring to many at first sight.

All the windows were placed high up so that it is unlikely that the garden could have been seen from inside; finally, very few seats are visible so it would appear that the girls had mainly to stand during their assemblies. As a regular illustration for the Report it was in strange contrast to the quite jolly photos of groups of mistresses or girls to be found in each issue of the School magazine.

One should not overlook a pleasant gesture being made by the railway at this period of private enterprise, namely that annually the London and South Western Railway Company is thanked for allowing 'the Pupils and Mistresses to travel on their line for the holidays with return tickets for single fares' – for those who might have lived at Plymouth or Portsmouth this would have been a most worthwhile concession. There is however no evidence that it applied to other railways.

The year 1910 brought, for the first time, two successes in London Matriculation and sixteen in various classes of the Oxford Local. Music was thriving too, with eleven passes and, for the first time there is a violin candidate; so far, all music seems to have been concentrated on the piano; enthusiasm for recorders is still some half century ahead. A general report by an outside examiner a year or so later indicates that the standard of Latin and Maths in the School could be raised slightly but the levels in Scripture, English, French, German and History were all good.

The generous Mr. Mullens gave as his 'treat' to the School the expenses of their visit to the Coronation Procession of George V and Queen Mary in the summer of 1911. It must have been a wonderful experience: the girls had to be in their places by 8 a.m. and they left Richmond Station by the 6.25 train – no door-to-door motor coach trips then – and two commissionaires were laid on to pilot the party from Victoria Station to their seats at the Victoria Memorial. The magazine stated: 'they had been given to us by His Majesty King George, who in spite of the many State engagements which must have followed each other so fast since his father's death, remembered the School of which he had been President . . . . In 1909 he sent us his birthday cake, and this fresh kindness made us feel we had, perhaps, a more personal cause than others for rejoicing at his coronation.'

The long interval between 10.30 when the gilded coach drawn by its eight cream coloured horses left the Palace, and 3.0 p.m. when it returned with the crowned King and Queen, passed very quickly for the girls who obviously took a thoroughly intelligent interest in all that went on. Hester Fligg, reporting for 'The Victory' gave an excellent, lively description of the scene in the Mall, the soldiers mainly in scarlet, the many Indians 'with their strange head-dress', the piling of arms whilst they were 'fallen out' – until the dramatic moment when each sprang to his post again and 'without any noticeable orders every man was in his place as a dull roar of cheering could be heard . . . . ' with the returning procession. They returned to the School at 5.30 after 'one of the most thrillingly enjoyable days of our lives' and surely one which they never forgot.

In the following year it was found that the Chapel organ was in need of a thorough overhaul, the organ builders inferring that 'if you do anything with it you must do the lot'. The likely cost was to be £80 and it is much to the credit of the School that mistresses and girls turned to and ran a bazaar at St. Margaret's on what proved to be a perfect July Saturday. Once again the magazine description evokes the scene: 'There were four stalls in the large Schoolroom furnished with the most expensive contributions. These included beautifully worked, deliciously comfortable looking cushions, artistically painted table centres, an exquisitely silk embroidered needlework picture, articles in leather work, as well as novel and pretty ornaments of all sorts and sizes'. A main feature was a packed stall of babies' and young children's clothes – also dolls, pin cushions and work baskets [a veritable feast of 'arts and crafts'!] . . . . and when you needed sustenance there were 'dainty teas served under the copper beech at moderate prices' (doubtless by the girls as waitresses). This alone should have been sufficient reward for any gallant father who might have given up his Saturday afternoon to the Good Cause. There were also concerts in the Hall and at the end of it all the magazine description ends proudly:

The following statement speaks for itself:

Proceeds	£87	15	6d
Repairing Organ etc	76	16	9
Balance used for further improving the chapel	£10	18	9

It was altogether a very fine effort (worth at least £800 in to-day's money) in which many Old Girls had also participated and it must have been a great satisfaction for everyone when, in the following term they were able to enjoy the full qualities of their organ once more. Built by the famous firm of William Hill, it is a most pleasant two-manual instrument of good tone. After surviving six years of the 1939 War in the deserted Chapel at St. Margaret's it was safely moved to Haslemere and, after a period in the Gym, it was installed in the new Chapel of the Kilmorey block where it continues to give good service. See p. 112.

The last Report of the Committee, before the life of the School was shaken by the 1914 War, recorded several good items. The Examiner under the Oxford Examination Delegacy, F. G. Brabant of Corpus Christi, stated 'the general work of the School is of a high character, and most of the results are excellent'. Of the 24 candidates entered for the Oxford Locals, as many as 18 obtained Honours, the rest passing. Among those Honours were six First Classes, the highest number in any previous year having been two.

The School was full up throughout the year and was in need of more accommodation, though from the financial standpoint there was the continuing problem that barely a tenth of the pupils were being paid for at the full rate.

The Prize Day in November 1913 was given special distinction by the presence of Princess Louis of Battenburg who was accompanied by the First Sea Lord, Admiral Prince Louis of Battenburg. Forty-two years later their younger son, the Earl Mountbatten of Burma, was to become the School's President, later to be succeeded by their great granddaughter Princess Anne.

An otherwise good year did however bring one disturbing item: the resignation of Miss Stone, who left to be married, and there was then no question of a married woman continuing to teach. It was impossible to speak too highly of the work she had done for St. Margaret's and she carried with her 'the best wishes of all concerned in its management'. Unquestionably Miss Stone fulfilled the expectations of her original appointment and after her ten years the School stood on an altogether higher plane both for its educational achievements and the general 'tone' of its girls. She was succeeded by Miss Fayerman, Cambridge Mathematical Tripos, Senior Optime, who came from Cheltenham Ladies College with the highest recommendations, and was to prove an admirable selection for the anxious years which lay ahead.

CHAPTER V

THE FIRST WORLD WAR

AUGUST 4th 1914, with all its implications, brought great anxiety to the School management most of whom had doubtless greater realisation than most people of what would be involved. However, it was quickly seen that their duty was – more than ever – to ensure that a good education should still be provided for the daughters of Naval Officers. Many more were, alas, likely to be rendered fatherless as the war proceeded. So the decision was made to carry on at Twickenham; at that stage the idea of air-raids on civilian populations was in England almost non-existent save, perhaps, in the mind of Mr. H. G. Wells.

Opportunity was taken to impress upon the girls a sense of patriotism and duty; to explain what the War meant to them individually and, as time went on to give calm and accurate accounts of the progress of the War from day to day. As with most organizations at that stage it was, quite sensibly, 'business as usual'.

As ever, finance for the School was not easy; ordinary subscriptions dropped away still further but there were certain windfalls to compensate. Lord Iveagh handed over to the School a substantial part of the sum paid to him by the Government for the wartime chartering of his magnificent yacht and they also received part of the £1000 generously raised by the Falkland Islands for England's War Charities. Then, in October 1915, the School President, Admiral of the Fleet Sir Hedworth Meux made a magnificent appeal in the form of a letter to several papers pointing out how inevitably the need for the purposes of the School must grow rapidly and that, at the same time, the cost of running it must increase. This produced over £6000 and enabled some important plans to go ahead at once.

Drains still needed attention, the antiquated hot water system had to be renewed, while the laundry required much up-to-date equipment, not only for its efficient use but also because the girls were to have instruction in laundry work! From this age of the automatic washing machine in the home it is difficult to envisage just what the 'young ladies' – as they were always called by the domestic staff – *would* have learnt from the particular machinery required for the washing of several hundred garments a week. At all events this was part of the very sound innovation to devote some of the School time to the teaching of general housewifery.

Mention of this in 'The Victory' gives scope for amusing descriptions of a girl's attempts at 'black-leading' a fireplace (essential job then with open coal fires) wherein much of the surrounding territory received an unnecessary blacking! But it was a good idea in days when every middle class home normally had at least one 'living-in' maid and very few girls had to do any washing up or cleaning, let alone try their hands seriously at cooking. In view of the much greater opportunities for women to work in factories which developed during the War, and their subsequent reluctance to go into domestic 'service', the School showed, perhaps unconscious foresight in preparing pupils for running their future homes single-handed.

This very point had been stressed by more than one Old Girl who had migrated to Canada: it was emphasised that life in the Western part of the country was still a hard struggle, that the 'slavey', as the poor maid-of-all-work was often termed here, just did not exist, and girls going to Canada simply must be trained to domestic work if they were to live and maintain a household comfortably. Much of this would have been revolutionary to their Mammas, though many of *them* were forced – often painfully – to learn the same skills for themselves as the War went on. It must be added that at least one of the courageous emigrants was firmly of the opinion that tough as was her life overseas, it offered her far more success and happiness than she would have expected in England. There, one would like to think, was the real fruit of one aspect of her RNS education.

The effects of war were soon evident. A long list of husbands and brothers of Old Girls on Active Service was published as well as many fathers of the girls at School. 'The Victory' carried a remarkable account, by one Old Girl, of several months spent in Holland during the first winter of the War, after she and her mother had been summoned to the bed-side of her father who was gravely ill when he was landed there after his ship, the *Hogue,* had been torpedoed. It comes as a strange reminder of the vastly different conditions for civilians in 1914 by comparison with those of Hitler's War.

At the School, girls worked away at the production of a number of garments for a new Services Hospital at Isleworth. As an immediate economy the Speech Day in November 1915 was simplified and no invitations were sent out. Still, there was a sizeable gathering, 24 prizes and 15 Oxford Local Certificates were distributed. A concert followed including the immortal 'Sur le Pont d'Avignon' – with action! – sung by Forms III and II and Sophie Facey, a senior, achieved Grieg's 'Wedding Day' at the piano after which the girls were allowed to go out with their friends and there was *dancing,* presumably among themselves – there was no mention of a male invasion. Whether this was the direct result of Miss Fayerman's new reign one does not know, but it must have come as a delightful liberation to the girls.

By the winter of 1915–16 Zeppelin Drill was being taken seriously though there had been no bombs near them. In the early evening all lights were put out, girls had to make their way up to their bedrooms, don dressing gowns and slippers, grab the red blanket from their beds and then descend to the lowest passages, mistresses being on guard at strategic points taking names to be sure no one was left behind in the bedrooms 'to the tender mercies of a German bomb'. When all were safely down there came the soothing words 'Now go and get supper'.

Touching on the matter of food again, and indicating the odd ups and downs of that period, one learns that their President Admiral Meux did not forget them when, surprisingly enough, he had the chance to get in some shooting. 'A gift of pheasants' came to the School and was greatly appreciated . . . how many brace, one longs to know . . . how did the School cook and serve them? How much did each girl get? It was typical of the kindness shown towards the School by more than one of its busy male benefactors.

War was not allowed to interfere with the good programmes of organised games which appeared to be thriving after – if not before – 1914. Matches with other schools were played regularly at tennis, cricket and hockey and there was also some basket ball. The first two feature at one of the Old Girls' days when they defeated the School at tennis but were beaten at cricket, doubtless getting less practice at the latter once they had left. A spirited performance of that old favourite *The Rivals* is given one summer and the Lower School contribute *Babes in the Wood*. One may regard it as all standard for many a girls' school in our time but it must be seen as a real 'break through' for St. Margaret's in that far-off period and it well may have owed something to the indirect influence of that Headmistresses' Association.

Miss Fayerman showed her quality and far-sightedness in an article she wrote for 'The Victory' in 1916 drawing attention to the enormously increased opportunities of employment for women, in worthwhile careers, which the War was bringing about. Prophetically she pointed out that after the War taxation would remain high, that living would be hard and that women would have special demands made upon them as earners. She doubtless foresaw that there would be many fewer parents able to support 'daughters at home' and she struck a fine note in her plea for a 'duty of service . . . . not confined to hospital work or handicraft, nor will it lie for all of us in the way of wifehood and motherhood'. She looked forward to matriculation at 16, and two more years of greater specialization. Then she most ardently recommended University, if possible, mentioning particularly Medicine and Teaching – the latter 'one of the finest and most exacting of the vocations open to women'. Miss Fayerman went on to survey the possibilities of a wide range of careers covering Pharmacy, Optics, Librarianship, Gymnastics, Massage, Domestic Science and Nursing of all kinds. The list is very much wider to-day and careers for women are a matter of course but before the dawn, even, of the Nineteen Twenties, this article showed vision.

After that issue with its 42 pages and two happy illustrations of Old Girls pursuing their vocations, one looking splendid in her nurse's uniform at a Military Hospital in Lincoln (surrounded by soldiers) and another showing a young mother with her two pretty children, we come to a sadly attenuated magazine for 1918. Inevitably the paper is thin and of poor quality, and there are only 24 pages. After the Battle of Jutland, in particular, the Roll of Honour is prominent, with nineteen deaths in action, nearly all of them brothers of Old Girls. The Speech Day was, however, carried through with a most distinguished educationist present, Miss Jex-Blake, Mistress of Girton, and she, not surprisingly also spoke on the subject of the work of girls in war-time and the need for a sound education.

In that year came the first reference to a serious concern for Science teaching when the Infirmary was 'fitted up temporarily' as a Laboratory. A further step in modernisation, and a move towards more self-government was a re-organisation of their Prefect system under which, in addition to the existing six Prefects, there were six Bedroom Monitresses who enjoyed some but not all of the full Prefectorial privileges.

An amusing feature of one War term was the arrival of two enormous packets from Queen Mary's Needlework Guild after which the whole school 'appeared to be full of grey wool' as the entire company set about knitting it up into cardigans for the troops. On the whole, it was said, the School seemed rather sorry when the work was finished. Meanwhile the allotment craze also spread to them and scientific digging and planting produced many rows of carrots and cabbages.

Apart from the five pages of news from Old Girls, indicating that most of them are doing useful jobs related in some way to the War, the magazine is not over-loaded with references to it and one has the clear impression that the work of the School is well maintained at a normal pitch.

The Committee's Report for 1918 records a most important development of the previous year. It began with the realisation that the School must be en-larged, for three main reasons:

1. That as a result of the War it was most desirable to make provision for an increased number of Officers' daughters to be able to attend.

2. To keep abreast of modern standards of education it was essential to in-crease the number of class rooms and the general facilities of the School.

3. It had become increasingly obvious that the number of pupils was low in relation to the Staff. 'The number of the latter could not be reduced without loss of efficiency but twenty more girls could receive education at the School without any increase in the number of teachers'.

The Committee had put its finger upon a vital spot, this time a fundamental truth of business, namely, that if you can increase 'sales' – in this case pupils – without adding to your overhead costs, you are sure to increase your margin. Thus they were to be able to keep down fees and so have more money available for building.

War-time inflation and shortage of materials and labour made it impossible to contemplate the actual work at that stage but the idea was born, some money was already in hand and determined efforts were made to increase the building fund over the next two or three years. The whole project represented one more act of faith for the School management, especially when the outcome of the War itself was still uncertain.

Appeals by two distinguished admirals, Sir Hedworth Meux and later Sir John Jellicoe and others had altogether raised over £12,000 and to this was added £5000, a wonderful gesture from the people of Canada, which came to the School via the Royal Patriotic Fund (for which it will be remembered the School still took five girls who were educated for only £5 a year). To perpetuate the memory of this generous gift, when an extension was eventually built it was named 'Canada House'. To this day part of the Haslemere complex of buildings is so-called, actually the Sanatorium, and many a new-comer has been perplexed to hear a girl say casually that she is 'going over to Canada'!

The sum aimed at for completion of their building scheme was £50,000 but they came near enough to it to enable the plans to be carried out. In May 1918, with a final appeal, the Report concluded with words which must have made a deep impression upon many:

'It is hoped that every person who reads this report will consider for a moment what they owe to the Officers of the Navy in return for their devotion to duty during the past three and a half years'.

The terrible epidemic of so-called Spanish influenza struck St. Margaret's later and less severely than was the case with many schools. Not until the autumn of 1918 did they have the 'visitation' with all the disturbance to routine, the nursing and the anxiety which came as such an added burden to so many school staffs just as they were hoping for some relief after four gruelling years. Unlike some schools – which had to break up early – they were able to keep going throughout that term. Apart from this the general health of the School appeared to remain remarkably good despite the poor quality of much of the food during the 1914 War when rationing was much less efficient than during the 1940s.

Two Reminiscences of life at the School during that War appeared in the 'Centenary Magazine' of 1940, the first by Miss Fayerman herself, and a much shorter piece by one of the maids of the time, Mollie Moody. Both in their different ways bring to mind so vividly the details and the atmosphere of the period – and the pluck with which the School faced them – that they are re-printed here.

'In the present struggle (1940) it is the tempo that dazes us, even if we are in the home front. Not so in the Great War; pressure was slow, if relentless; it was the last twelve months of it in which the screw turned so tightly.

For a long time normal life at RNS was little altered. Black-out roller blinds appeared at the windows. No diminution in individual plumpness seemed apparent at any time, though margarine began to make its appearance (and how angry the staff were when they found they had eaten it at certain meals for three weeks without knowing it!), and Mrs Shales, housekeeper of famous memory had to be restrained from increasing the three-days'-old stage for the consumption of bread to five days, or in extreme cases even six. England was very slow to introduce rationing, and some foods became very hard to get, and prices terribly high; it took two secretaries and hours of telephoning to obtain three or four big jars of jam, or a chest of tea. In later stages, an egg became a meal of great luxury, and cheese was often unobtainable. When rationing began, it was in respect of meat, fats, butter, and margarine, lard, bacon, and sugar; there were no reliefs for "catering establishments", but there were endless clippings of coupons by the hundred. A person who obtained more than one ration book or wrongly held it was liable to a fine of £100. There was a dreadful moment when we could obtain no lard at all, and our ample cook, "after all the years I've been here, Miss Fayerman," was in despair as to how to produce the fruit tarts that were the time-honoured essential to the whole School's Sunday dinner. We strove, we racked our brains, and as a last resort we got hold of some olive

a

Miss A. E.
Chaplin
(1919–1933).
'The Skipper'
affectionately
known also
as 'Charlie'.

b

Miss W. M. Fayerman who saw the
RNS through the First War
(1914–1919).

c

A girl of 1919.
Dorothea Bluett
(now Lady Hamilton).

Stoatley, the terrace which overlooks
the Weald.

The entrance hall with portrait of
Adl. Sir Thomas Williams.

October 1951, Admiral Sir Arthur Hall lays the stone of the new Kilmorey block
watched by Miss Oakley-Hill, the Rev. Gordon Shelford
and the architect, Mr. Bostock.

oil and made the pastry with that. We never did it again, for it was so hard that we nearly broke our teeth; but it was a gesture; and I daresay it saved cook's reason. I still have my last ration book, dated November, 1918; it says, "Grow potatoes if you can; the nation cannot have too many." We all dug a great bed in the lawn near the front door, and grew vegetables ourselves, under the direction of Earles, our clever, good-tempered gardener.

There were sad days, when war news was heavy, or when there came tidings of personal loss. On the morning when the news of the Battle of Jutland came I was already on my way to a Headmistresses' Conference in London, but turned back, knowing it must be a day of sorrow. The pluck of those daughters or sisters I shall never forget.

There were no trench shelters then, and the air-raid menace assailed us, generally by night; and down would come the School to range itself along the inner walls of corridors, clad in dressing-gowns and blankets, and we would play games, or sing, or tell stories through the night, till the all-clear signal released us. Drinks and biscuits would be consumed, and we would lie in bed till a later hour next day. On one occasion we were downstairs for long periods for three nights on end, and felt rather like chewed string at the end of it. We became intimately acquainted with each other's dressing-gowns, and knew how the staff's hair looked when it was down – for hair grew long in those days. Some of the children took the vigils lightly, but it was those who sang the loudest and whose eyes were brightest, whose gallantry one recognised, and whose strain one unobtrusively tried to ease. Often, on summer nights, with one or other of the staff, I would go into the garden and hear gunfire rolling up from the coast, steadily nearer and nearer, a fine but awful sound; and once we saw a blazing streak fall from the sky, and learnt next day that a Zeppelin had crashed at Billericay.

Getting about became tiresome. The tubes were crowded by nightfall, as refuges; walls and courts of London's lovely buildings, e.g. of Lincoln's Inn, were pock-marked with the "scatter" of bombs; and one day, in 1917, Londoners saw the Stars and Stripes floating at Westminster beside the Union Jack – America had come in at last.

The faithfulness of established members of the staff was a great comfort, but, near the end, new staff came and went rapidly, indeed, the difficult shortage of teachers remained till long after the Armistice. As for maids, they became priceless; conscience went to the winds, and visitors to the School would say enticing words to any maid who came near them. At the worst moment we obtained four young Irish maids, who were like gazelles for shyness, beauty and innocence – they had never left home before; and one of these, Mollie, became for years one of the School's best friends.

Throughout the autumn of 1918 strain and underfeeding caused a national epidemic of influenza, of a type that specially attacked young folks, and that tended to pass with fatal ease into pneumonia. Although we did not have the scourge as badly as many schools, we had one serious bout of it, and the spirit of one little girl – Irene – even on Peace Day, November 11th, returned to God who gave it. When the maroons sounded at 11 o'clock, Miss Kynoch was crossing Richmond Bridge, and a tiny boy accosted her. "Them's the maroons, that's for Peace", he said. "Yes", said she. "And father's dead at home", went on the child. What could one do? To us it was a day of infinite sadness. But London seethed with excitement. I had occasion to cross Hammersmith Broadway at about midday; all cars, taxis, drays, were seized, swarmed over, driven anywhere and by anyone; the crowd was a law unto itself.'

A Maid's Memories of the War

'There were then five housemaids, one acting as house-parlourmaid, cook, and two kitchenmaids.

The young ladies used to clear their own dining-room tables and help to lay up occasionally. They took domestic lessons by turning out one or two dormitories, or sometimes a mistress's bedroom.

The floors were all scrubbed in those days. At half-term the maids had to go up at nine o'clock at night to scrub some of the classrooms; then the housekeeper brought up tea to them. I remember seeing one young lady scrubbing down the back staircase, using her silk dressing gown for a kneeling mat. I said "Miss, you will ruin your dressing gown"; but she answered and said, "Oh, anything in war time!" That was the spirit they had to help to win the war.

It was hard to get maids, since most of them were doing munition work. Once the cook was sick for a day or two, and the Principal came down and asked me for a morning apron, as she was going to help to cook the dinner. She made some treacle tarts, which were a great treat in those days.

I helped to get the staff dinner one night, which consisted of boiled eggs and Queen of Puddings. I also made rock cakes for the children's tea.

Another one of my jobs was to see that each young lady had an equal share of jam, so I put a teaspoonful on each plate. Tea was served once a day at tea time, and cans of cocoa for breakfast. The Sixth Form used to have their breakfast in the Staff dining-room with the Head Mistress and Music Mistress; the rest of the staff sat at the head of each of the six tables. Sometimes, when meat was short, we substituted for it vegetable soup and steam pudding, also when potatoes could not be produced, broad beans were used instead.

In 1918 the bad epidemic of 'flu raged; there were only a few left in the School who did not have it; those who were left helped to carry up the trays to the top corridor. Many of the teachers took it, also the housekeeper and Sister in charge, and maids. There were many changes in hospital nurses, for they no sooner came than they had to go away again with the 'flu.

Then came Armistice Day and the national flag was put up on the Big gates. There was rejoicing outside, but the School was very sad, as one of our little girls died of 'flu at one o'clock that day.

Years passed on to 1923 and much improvement began. Electric lights were fitted, as there were only gas jets in dormitories, and an oil reading lamp in the drawing room. Floors were all stained and polished. New floors were made in the front hall and classrooms. The old laundry was made into the D.S.K. instead of using half a cupboard in the lounge where cleaning utensils were kept. Cooking lessons were taken outside the School. The older girls of the Sixth Form had a sitting-room made out of the old clinic, which is now a maids' bathroom. The School had been gradually growing through this time, and two more houses had been opened.

The present young ladies have a much better time in every way than those of the past.'   MOLLIE MOODY

A final memory of war days, this from one who was a schoolgirl then: 'I came to RNS during the last part of the War and am constantly thinking of those days – air-raids, rations and the food itself! I think very dry porridge, with suspicious looking brown sand and no milk is what I remember most, and most disliked: it was a spartan breakfast, and in those days one ate everything with no excuses. Is it fair, I wonder, to remember one member of the School who spent a very long day in the Library with a plate of porridge as sole company? She rejoined us after supper with a wicked twinkle in her eye, and later confided to us that the porridge was in a vase on the mantelpiece! Bread rations were another trial – two and a half rounds only for tea, and how quickly they went! And how firm a certain Mollie Moody was when we dared to ask for more. I remember how we hungry ones could claim the bread of those of more dainty appetite; immediately Grace was said, it would be, 'Bags your extra round, So-and-so'. We were a greedy crowd. A cup of milk and a round of bread and dripping or margarine was supper in those days – and cold blue cocoa for breakfast. . . . But how we flourished on it! I can remember my fattest days were at RNS.'

Readers old enough to have been at school themselves in 1918 may feel that the writer is unjust to herself and her fellows in accusing them of greed. The hunger which could come upon growing girls and boys at a time when meat, fats and bread were all scarce, was truly memorable, yet, as she infers, they managed to put on weight in spite of it all. What few children could realize at the time was the enormous amount of extra effort, ingenuity and sheer hard work put in by school Principals and their domestic staff to produce even the 'beastly food' which was served, and to keep the whole organization running. It was one more test which St. Margaret's did not fail.

CHAPTER VI

THE NINETEEN-TWENTIES

IN 1919 came, inevitably, an increase in the full-rate fees. It was an achievement on the part of successive Committees and Lady Principals that, although facilities had steadily improved, the fees had remained unaltered since the late 1870s, but now they moved up to £70 a year and *pro rata* for the intermediate scales. The crucial 'Foundation' rate, however, remained at £12 per annum and continued to represent astonishing value for those in real need. At the same time they bore still more heavily, in proportion, upon the School's finances. While dealing with the question of fees, opportunity was taken to put up the rate for the daughters of civilians to £120 which was about the normal for an unendowed boarding school, furthermore there must have been many fathers in the professional classes who had not been eligible for service in the forces and were able to pay this higher scale.

The Appeal Fund continued to grow and many unusual, and historically interesting, sources are shown, e.g. Queen Alexandra's Rose Day (for so many years a rather charming feature when that Queen herself would drive through many London streets in an open horse-drawn carriage to visit and encourage the rose-sellers). This fund gave £100 to the RNS, the Mercers Company £250, the East Indies Station Naval Fund made a second contribution of £565 and there came a useful share of the proceeds from the Exhibition of 'Mystery Ships' and captured German submarines. Thus, by the end of 1919, it became possible to complete the improvement of the central heating – a great boon – and to install electric light.

Then, in January 1920, came the surprising announcement of Miss Fayerman's resignation on her acceptance of the headship of Tonbridge County School. Her departure was much regretted by the Committee, who recorded her magnificent service over six trying years, and the way in which she had kept the School abreast of every modern movement.

Inevitably one speculates on the reasons behind her move: in terms of status one imagines that St. Margaret's would have ranked well above a County School but the Tonbridge appointment might then have carried a higher salary with a guaranteed pension at a stated age; also Miss Fayerman may well have been one who did not believe in remaining too long in one job at her comparatively early age and probably she saw the County Schools as a particularly interesting and challenging development for the future.

Her successor, a woman of outstanding character and ability, was Miss A. E. Chaplin, B.Sc., of Cheltenham Ladies College and as there was a hiatus apparently during the Spring term, before she could take up her duties an earlier Headmistress kindly offered her services temporarily. She was the former Miss Stone who had ruled so successfully from 1904-1914 when she left to be married; tragically, her husband, Dr. Fowler, had died within a few months and, though Mrs. Fowler appears not to have returned to teaching, she had edited the RN School magazine and had thus kept fully in touch. The inter-regnum passed off easily and Miss Chaplin began in the summer of 1920, bringing several new members of Staff with her to replace some who had left.

The examination results took on a new pattern with five successes in the London Matriculation, five School Certificates besides eight in the familiar Oxford Senior Local, all of which represented a healthy proportion in relation to the size of the School.

There remained the usual struggle to balance accounts for the year 1919 which ended with a deficit of £371. Comparing the total cost of two major items of expenditure in 1919, with those of 1915, one is left marvelling that the loss was not much worse:

Teachers' salaries rose from £969 to £1253

Food from £850 to £1590

only the increase in fees, coupled with the greater number of pupils had saved the situation, receipts here having risen from £2237 to £3192.

It is immediately clear that the salaries were not keeping pace with the cost of food (and doubtless with the cost of living generally) but this was to be remedied soon and within seven years that particular item was more than doubled. A very pronounced wind of change was about to strike the educational world as a result of the famous Education Act, 1918, the work of H. A. L. Fisher, then President of the Board of Education. One outcome of it was the Burnham Committee, under the chairmanship of Lord Burnham, which evolved a regular salary scale for qualified teachers coupled with a pension scheme. Ruth Chignell, then a teacher in her forties, wrote an excellent article about it in *The Victory*.

Pointing out that, whereas in her girlhood teaching was almost the only career open to women, there was by 1920 a far wider range of opportunities. Thus it was essential to make the profession much more attractive than formerly: the new Women's Training Colleges offered a two-year course at moderate fees and after completing it successfully a girl could begin at once to earn £150 a year. In ten years she could expect possibly as much as £320 and a great deal more if she became the head of a school. That these were then seen as attractive figures is a stark reminder of the extremely poor pay that teachers had received hitherto.

Around £40 a year had been the anticipated level in 1840 and even by 1913 the total teachers' salaries bill in St. Margaret's was just under £1000, spread over fifteen of them and including the headmistress! Allowing substantially more for her, but less for the visiting 'professors', it probably worked out at an average of no more than £60 for the resident mistresses in addition to their board and lodging. Even with the multiplication by at least ten (some might say nearer twenty) for a rough comparison with the value of money today, it was poor remuneration for educated women with considerable responsibilities – even if they did enjoy long holidays. At the start the scheme covered only what were then termed Elementary Schools but it was expected soon to cover all schools in the land. This came about, in due course (some schools paying well above the new scale) but there was an uncomfortable stage during which many felt themselves unable to pay the Burnham Scale and teachers had to choose between taking an appointment in the school of their first choice or going to another, of perhaps lesser status, which had accepted the new scale.

Miss Chignell expressed the hope that many RNS girls might feel drawn to teaching in the future and ended with an impressive definition of the job and the qualities needed for it: 'The work is harder than many other forms of work, in that one has to put one's own *personality* into it if there is to be any success; also one needs constant good temper, a sense of humour, resourcefulness and a keen sense of justice, in addition to the book-learning required; and no girl should enter the profession if she is not prepared to cultivate all these. But, if the work is hard, the interest of it is infinite and the holidays are sufficiently good in all schools to give one a chance for rest and recuperation. There is little doubt that the lot of the teachers of the future is going to be a great deal better than it has been for those in the past.' One is happy to think that this prophecy has been abundantly fulfilled over the ensuing half century.

In 1920 there was still a 'shortage of maids' and the girls continued to do a certain amount of house-work, though not so much as in the Spring : it seems probable that they never again had quite the quality of reliable and kindly retainers who bore so much of the burden of domestic chores before 1914. Meanwhile the marriage rate went steadily forward with eight recorded in the Magazine for that year, five of them, not surprisingly, to naval officers. Other news of old girls showed a wide selection of jobs being tackled: one sets up as a taxi-driver in Malvern, investing in her own taxi, her mother keeping the accounts and answering the telephone. Two still do military nursing, one of them awarded the Mons 1914 Star and the Queen Elizabeth Belgian Medal, the other goes on to work as a masseuse in Winnipeg. Maternity Training, Dairy Work, Poultry and Bees claim others and one young lady has done well on the stage, playing the lead at the famous Gaiety Theatre in *Going Up*.

It shows enterprise and adaptability and from the scholastic standpoint the most impressive is a letter from Dorothy Torlesse who describes her 'absolutely delightful' life at Girton College, Cambridge. She rightly felt very proud to be the first RNS girl there but was already looking forward to the arrival of a second, Nancy Wickham, who was to come up the following October. Since then RNS girls have continued to obtain places at the Oxford and Cambridge colleges in numbers which, though small, significantly reflect the consistent maintenance of the highest academic standards at the School.

By 1921 the Committee faced the consequences of the Fisher reforms which made it clear that, to obtain an efficient Teaching Staff, it was desirable for them to secure 'recognition' of the School under the School Teachers (Superannuation) Act 1918. Like many others at the time they had to agree to submit the School to the close scrutiny of Board of Education Inspectors who, after a visitation of several days, expressed themselves as satisfied with the efficiency of the School as an educational establishment. One dare not speculate what some members of the Committee must have thought to themselves about all this but they wisely decided – as King George V did later with his first Labour Government – to 'march with the times'.

Their good friend Mr. Mullens continued his imaginative hospitality with a London Matinée, and tea after it, for the entire School which was, once more, 'much enjoyed', and must indeed have been one of his most expensive treats. Incidentally as a note of historic interest, in 1922 for his whole day picnic to Virginia Water, he utilised for the first time the 'motor Char-à-banc' – the open vehicle with transverse seats, all facing forwards, which seemed in its day ideal for the country outing in summer, much more fun than the all-enclosed motor coach. Plainly it was a huge success, what with the char-à-bancs loaded with urns of lemonade and baskets of food, then the drive, the picnic lunch, exploring expeditions, and a visit to Holloway College (for Women), 'enjoyment knew no bounds'!

The following year saw the numbers moving steadily up though it was only by additional day-girls that the School could grow at this stage. They numbered 26 so that the total was then 108.

With the customary long waiting list for boarding places, it was clear to the Committee that additional accommodation was required and that a continuing demand for it could be confidently anticipated. The matter had in fact been considered the previous year when it had been decided that, rather than attempting to build an extension to the original School House (which would have been an awkward and costly undertaking), they would purchase an adjoining property, Gordon House, and its grounds, which gave them an extra eight acres to bring up the School total to fourteen acres, making a very fine area for games and athletics generally.

The property was formally acquired in July 1923 and such was the speed of building and decoration work at the time that, within ten weeks, the new House was ready for occupation for the Autumn term at the end of September. At the same time, despite all-round rising costs they managed to achieve a small balance on the right side so had no need to dip into reserves.

The original Gordon House dated back to 1680 and underwent alterations by its various owners, one of them employing Robert Adam as architect. A print of 1829 shows it as a charming 18th century style of country house, beautifully sited beside the river and sheltered from the north by well-placed trees. By 1869 a Victorian owner had laid his heavy hand upon it with extensions, pretentious decoration and an ugly little tower on the river side, which appeared to serve no useful purpose. It began to look rather like an orphanage, in the grand manner, and in fact that was virtually what it became in 1897 when the London School Board acquired it as one of the new certified Industrial Schools for Girls. In their day these institutions did good work in the rehabilitation and training of some of the 'waifs and strays' – the homeless and destitute youngsters who swarmed in parts of London eighty years ago. For various reasons, partly a breakdown in the health of the Superintendent and other staff difficulties, the school was closed in 1922.

Gordon House was at once made into the Junior House, able to accommodate 55 more girls and the necessary staff. It also provided space for a Science Room and a Domestic Science kitchen for seniors. Although its river frontage appeared rather forbidding with its tower, the opposite side of the house facing the garden, which ran out at ground floor level, looked very pleasant. It must have seemed a much more agreeable and less formidable house for juniors than was St. Margaret's. The first floor ceilings were not so lofty and it would have been easier to heat. The entrance hall was more like that of a friendly country house and the broad stairs, with their nicely carved balustrade and easy treads, were just made to sprint up two at a time – if girls were allowed to use them! There seems no doubt whatever that the acquisition of Gordon House was an excellent move which proved successful in every way.

Other interesting events of that period were further results of the Royal patronage of the School: in 1922 they were given seats near to Buckingham Palace to watch the Wedding Processions for the marriage of Princess Mary, daughter of King George V, to Viscount Lascelles, and in the following year Queen Mary herself visited the School once again. It was her first appearance since that time in 1893 when, as a quite young woman and soon after her marriage, she had come to St. Margaret's with her mother, the Duchess of Teck.

The object of the present visit was the opening of the new Junior School building, Gordon House. The occasion was well reported in all the local papers and a photograph showed Her Majesty with the characteristic fur muff of the period and Miss Chaplin, in gown and hood, at her side. The *Sunday Times* gave it nearly half a column:

'. . . the Queen was received on arrival by the president of the school, Admiral Sir Hedworth Meux, and was conducted to her place at the head of a flight of broad shallow steps in the old hall.

'On one side of the hall were assembled a large company of guests and on the other side the pupils of the Senior School, whose white silk blouses and navy blue skirts stood out in sharp relief against the old oak of the furnishings. At the entrance of Her Majesty, who looked very charming in blue with a pale mauve hat, the children sang the National Anthem. A number of visitors and members of the staff were presented to the Queen by Admiral Meux. To each Her Majesty said a few words and appeared delighted when the head girl, Barbara Handley, handed her a bouquet of crimson carnations, bound with a broad ribbon of navy blue silk, thus embodying the School colours.'

The Queen was then conducted on a tour of the Senior School, proceeding afterwards to the new Junior School where she formally declared the building open.

'Her Majesty had intended to leave immediately after the inspection but, having seen the excellently equipped kitchen, she decided to take tea with Miss Chaplin . . . Her Majesty expressed her pleasure at all she had seen and her appreciation of the arrangements that had been made for the comfort and education of the children . . .'

A subsequent letter to the *Morning Post* stated that 'the honour of the visit, so intensely appreciated, gave the highest encouragement alike to the authorities of the School and the children who so happily welcomed her Majesty'. It must really have given a tremendous 'lift' to everyone, not least when the Queen followed it up a few days later with handsome, framed photographs of herself and the King and a gift of books for the School library.

Another gratifying result was that, to mark the honour of the Royal visit, Sir Edward Donner, Bt., presented the sum of £1000 (remember that would be £10,000 at least today) to the School, part of it to increase the endowment of the Donner Scholarship, in memory of his brother Capt. Charles Donner and the balance to be used as the Committee should decide. Others who responded to this memorable occasion in a similar practical fashion were Lord and Lady Louis Mountbatten. Altogether it was a splendid example of the many benefits which can accrue to an organization so fortunate as to enjoy royal patronage.

The one-time 'Lady Governess', succeeded by the 'Lady Principal', was at last designated as Head Mistress and Miss Chaplin appears thus in the Report for 1923; conceivably this was another indirect result of the royal visit! Also, at about the same time, there was the very sensible division of the School into three 'Houses' bearing the honoured names of Drake, Grenville and Nelson, of which the appointed house mistresses were, respectively Miss Hunt (Classics), Miss Castle (Domestic Science) and Miss Quale (Piano); thus new rivalries in sports, and in some aspects of work were intended to provide an extra stimulus. The 1923 Magazine includes photos of all three Houses, rather fuzzy, so that they all look identical dark figures except for Grenville where Miss Castle and Matron are resplendent in white blouse and uniform. The girls all appear rather grave in their blue serge dresses (like overalls) with white collars and, of course, skirts of generous length – the short ones of the later Twenties were yet to come.

The careers of the Old Girls were still more varied as they continued to expand into very much wider fields than those of the faithful governesses of the past. One is a secretary in Shanghai who revels in the short working hours and who refers quite shamelessly, as did so many English people then, to the 'chinks' (with not even a capital letter!). Another is a Norland nurse, a third an assistant school matron while yet one more is up at St. Hugh's, Oxford. An interesting modern note comes from one at Girton who is already engaged to a 4th year man at Glasgow University. It was all rather different from such news as filtered through in the days of the previous generations of RNS girls.

With these changes came another one of enormous relief and satisfaction to the Committee. The 1925 Report disclosed an almost unbelievable balance of £1900 Receipts over Expenditure. It was, of course, the fruit of good planning, as well as some good fortune: higher fees – more pupils – extra support from certain Funds which made distributions for naval objects – and stringent economy in everything not directly connected with the education and health of the girls. This was a fine achievement especially since the economies had been effected while it appeared that the general level of School life was growing fuller and more interesting.

Another significant feature of their accounts was that, thanks to the continued policy of adding to their Investment Fund wherever possible – with special donations as distinct from subscription – the investments were then valued at £33,000, producing an income of over £2000. However, there was always some new expenditure to be faced: part of the grounds of Gordon House had been let to a market gardener whose lease expired within two years. Wisely the Committee decided to take in the eight acres of land for use as additional playing fields so, once more, there went into their Report the firmly expressed hope 'that friends of the School will come forward to enable the grounds to be laid out without encroaching upon the invested Funds'.

More topical signs come into the records of 1925 when, once again the School's royal and naval connections produce an absolutely first-class outing: a visit to the Dress Rehearsal of the Royal Tournament at Olympia, that superb, ever-green display of British Servicemen at their smartest and most impressive. Fifty years ago the Naval guns were already being dismantled and rushed across that imaginary river, by hand, in miraculously short time! The girls could also have known the thrills of the Musical Ride at high speed by Cavalry describing intricate figures all over the arena.

Another day which, if tiring, must have been memorable for all of the girls was a visit to the 'British Empire Exhibition' at Wembley in 1924 at the generous invitation of Sir Charles Cust and Sir Henry Campbell. Financially and politically the Exhibition may not have been a great success but it was undoubtedly a fine 'show' at the time, with considerable educational value. Doubtless essays had to be written about it at St. Margaret's subsequently, and one enterprising young lady produced for *The Victory* Sir Roger de Coverley's impressions of *his* visit to Wembley.

Incidentally, the magazine also indicates advances in its Sports section. Line drawings liven up the subject headings and for tennis we have girls leaping about the court in really short cotton frocks with unmistakably Suzanne Lenglen style bandeaux on their heads – a big change from the sweeping dark serge skirts of their early tennis days. For hockey that searching feature, 1st Eleven Team 'characters', emerges where we learn that one player 'dribbles quickly and accurately' but another, alas, 'lacks speed, determination and finish' – the Captain, B. Hambly was tough with her team which in its early days did not seem to win many matches but never mind, the School now had all four games fully established and played regularly hockey, netball, cricket and tennis, with the added interest of House matches.

In the following year work on the new playing fields were well advanced and they were, in fact, completed by March 1927; with some of the original trees carefully preserved at the edges the area looked most attractive. There was now space for four full-sized tennis courts, the large pitch which could be used for lacrosse, as well as hockey and cricket, with room also for several practice nets, and a great advantage was that girls were no longer obliged to spend about 40 minutes of the time allowed for games in walking to and from the ground, previously hired for them, at Marble Hill, Twickenham. Such a practice was by no means unusual then for many a suburban or city school which often had its playing field a mile or more away.

There were now 125 boarders in the two Houses, plans were in hand for building a new Dormitory over the Junior House Playroom which would take ten more children; then, with 42 day girls added the total became 177 – more than double that of the early St. Margaret's – and was altogether more economic or, in to-day's jargon, 'viable'. Added to these very satisfactory figures was the waiting-list of more than 100; there was little fear that the additional accommodation was not going to be utilised to the full.

The Staff had grown considerably and, including Matrons, amounted to 27. By comparison with the War years it looked increasingly professional. After the Head, there was an official Second Mistress, Miss A. A. Mowat, with a Cambridge MA, all other mistresses of recognised subjects held the degree of BA, mainly London, the Music mistresses their LRAM. Each had a qualification for her speciality as far as Assistant Matron, Junior School, who was from the Hospital for Sick Children, Great Ormond Street. That War-time Staff of only 15, five of them visiting teachers, might well have looked askance at the number of their successors and at what would have seemed to be much sub-division of the jobs which individuals had managed to cope with in the past. But standards were rising all the time and it is doubtful whether any of the new generation of mistresses were working any less hard, or under less pressure, than did their predecessors.

By 1927 the Accounts once more plunged into 'the red' to the tune of £800 mainly because of the state of the floors in the School House which, by then, had borne some seventy years of hard wear. The original builder could hardly have anticipated the relentless pounding which his boards must have endured from a quite exceptional number of energetic young feet. In some places floors had become a positive 'danger to the children', and a major work of totally re-flooring the Senior Hall, the corridors and several classrooms was undertaken.

Then, with eyes firmly on the future, the School seized another good opportunity to expand. Ormonde Lodge, a somewhat ornate Victorian House adjoining the School property, with its half acre of garden, came on to the market and the Committee snapped it up. Giving room for 20 more pupils, it was a thoroughly sound purchase but the necessary alterations and re-decoration cost £3783. The building, re-named Hood House, was used for the younger girls for their first year, as an intermediate stage, before embarking upon the full routines of the main School; a successful effort was made to achieve a 'more homelike atmosphere' which was appreciated by both the girls and many of their parents. A slight curiosity, at the same time, was the decision to divide the new House into two parts, to be named Port and Starboard which hardly appears to engender the intended suggestion of 'home'.

To conclude the financial worries of the period there was the damage due to the serious flooding of the Thames in the Christmas holidays of 1927. It was caused by the conjunction of a flood tide and an exceptionally strong north easterly wind. In parts of London the river rose above the embankment walls, a great many basement dwellings were flooded and there was some loss of life as the high tide came at night. The effect was felt all the way up the tidal reach as far as Teddington Lock and this, of course, included St. Margaret's. The basement of the new Hood House was flooded as was Gordon House, and the ground floor of the Senior, while there was 3 feet of water in the Lodge, where two pianos were badly damaged. The most costly repair involved was probably that of the wall, alongside the river and immediately in front of the Junior House.

The weight of the water had pushed it badly out of the perpendicular and the wall had to be re-built. For the School it was a mercy that the flood had not occurred in their term time, at least there were not added anxieties for the welfare and safety of nearly 200 girls and staff as well as the laborious work of clearing up and 'making good'.

In other ways 1927 could be counted as a good year. Exam results came out well with 15 sitting for the General Schools of London University, 11 Passes, 6 with exemption from Matric and plans made for 23 girls to take it in the following year.

Much the most spectacular achievement was the really outstanding pageant, *The Story of Education.* written by Miss A. A. Mowat and Miss E. Hussey, House Mistress of Nelson. It was performed on Speech Day in the Autumn and altogether on nine other occasions during that term, thus giving to the enthusiastic young actresses that rare pleasure which so seldom comes to amateurs: several repeat performances so that the players can get well worked into their parts and able to enjoy them all the more.

Extracts from an account in *The Victory*, by two Sixth Formers M. Goodwin and A. Marsh, help to convey the spirit of what must have been a most splendid affair.

There were 18 Scenes tracing the History of Education from 2000 BC to the present day and the play also embodied a rough outline of the progress of music and dancing through the ages.

'After a short introduction by the Chronicler, who provided also a running commentary on the action, the curtain rose on a scene in which the children of Hood House, as Greeks, danced to their God, Pan. Next came a Jewish School where boys, in fez and coloured tunics knelt round the Rabbi as they learnt the first ten letters of the Hebrew alphabet. Then the Roman School:
> They speak in Latin, then a living tongue,
> Now dead, alas! save to the studious few . . .

Then to a scene in the half light of the cloisters of a Frankish monastery and a vesper hymn was heard above the drone of the novice master, teaching the novices to illuminate:
> After the fall of pagan Rome, the hand
> Of Mother Church assumed the sole control . . .

So, on to the training of a Squire under the Seneschal, to be followed by a Winchester scene:
> Founder of Winchester! William of Wykeham, he
> Whose precepts sound have since the School began
> Sent Wykhamists to teach a hurrying world
> The wholesome truth that 'Manners Makyth Man' . . .

After an Interval, the Post-Renaissance era was shown, the curtain rising on a class at St. Paul's School where Colet received a letter from Erasmus. After an address given by the latter to the 'Prentices in Learning' the 'boys' sang *Non Nobis Nomine!*

The Renaissance has waked men's minds to search:
The pages of the classics, long unread.
London's great School, where gentle Colet taught
Beneath the shadow of old St. Paul's . . .
So, to the court of Henry VIII and splendid scenes in Richmond Palace.
Later, after the Dame School where a poor but well meaning woman tried to teach village children:
To help the poor, and train the orphan child.
With good intentions but herself untrained . . .
there was the scene at Miss Pinkerton's Academy from *Vanity Fair:*
Once more to London, and in Chiswick Mall
Imagine that as guests you see the School:
Amelia Sedley . . . flouted Becky Sharp . . .
An age refined when affectation ruled,
And graces ousted all sincerity.
Then the Victorian School now coming rather near to home one feels!
. . . lessons here are learned
But never taught. Girls con the printed page,
Repeat by rote the knowledge thus imbibed.
The mistress neither knows nor cares to know
The nature of the pupil in her care . . .
and the final scene in 1902
But now a ray of glorious hope is seen
Gilding the future of the British girl . . .
See then the opening of a Public School,
The path of opportunity for girls . . .

This last was represented in tableaux form to show the numerous activities of modern education and finally there was the grand tableau consisting of groups of characters from each scene arranged in chronological order. The foregoing is part paraphrase of the original description and with only the briefest extracts from words of the Chronicler but it may serve to convey the attractiveness and ingenuity of the whole production which was properly staged and lit – thanks to the innovation of electricity in the School House.

The account of the Misses Goodwin and Marsh ended with a paragraph which should be quoted in full:

'The costumes, every one historically accurate, were with the lighting which showed them to best advantage, largely responsible for the success of the Play. For the former Miss Godden and Miss Chesterfield, organizing the labour of many skilled workers, were in charge, while we were lost in admiration of Miss Brackenbury's masterly manipulation of flex and switches. The beautiful music under Miss Chesterfield's direction, and the ballet and formal dances arranged by Miss Priestman spoke for themselves of the work which had been put into them.

'Miss Brinsmead, as property master controlled the congested traffic behind the scenes and through the office, Miss Ireland and Miss Jarrett were responsible for make-up; while here, there and everywhere at once, Miss Hussey stage-managed the whole production, filling everyone with her own enthusiasm.'

Standard acknowledgements, one may think, but it was a wholly new departure, in its scale and magnificence; such an undertaking had never before been attempted at St. Margaret's and one feels that those resourceful and intensely hard-working mistresses who 'got it all up' should be on record. Both Miss Mowat and Miss Hussey made great contributions to the life of the School, and the latter in particular, was to be closely identified with it over a long period, being made Second Mistress in succession to Miss Mowat in 1933. She was a remarkable lady of many talents, including considerable gifts for administration; she 'knew everything' about the School. She was ever approachable and remained, over some 25 years, the mistress above all others to whom girls could always turn when they had problems to discuss.

The decade of the 1920s ended with the deaths of three people who had, in their different spheres, rendered great service to the School. First there was Mr. G. Holt Stilwell who had been Honorary Treasurer for no less than 24 years – perhaps a seemingly unheroic and rather thankless task for it must have been his duty, time and again, to warn against expenditure which the Committee must have wished to undertake. Yet what a skilful achievement it must have been to have kept them on a reasonably even keel and to have managed to find the money as and when it was needed.

Within the same year they lost another pillar of the Committee, no less than Captain Henry Cavendish, RN, who had served them for 22 years, much of that time as Chairman. He had retired comparatively young from the Navy on his marriage to Lady Harriet Godolphin Osborne, sister of the Duke of Leeds, and he must have devoted a great deal of his time to the School, on the one hand to the detail of its management and on the other, to its relation with the Navy and to its other distinguished supporters. He must also have shown considerable tact to have dealt successfully with a Committee which usually comprised six or seven admirals and many other officers of a rank superior to that which he had held.

The third death which would have struck to the hearts of many, especially the seniors among the Old Girls, was that of Miss Leys. Though obliged to retire 25 years earlier, she had kept in touch and for many years had written a letter to each issue of *The Victory*, always beginning 'My dear Children'. A long and moving obituary in the magazine recalled the extreme difficulties of her early life. She had been left motherless in infancy, living for a time with her elder sister on board her father's ship at Chatham where her education was limited to memorising pages of *Mangnall's Questions* under the direction of her sister. Later there was a terrible little boarding school at Romsey from which she was rescued only by her father's early death, then the 'miracle' by which vigorous efforts by his brother officers secured her a place at the Royal Naval Female School (although she was barely within the age limit).

After leaving the School at 18, as Head Girl, she worked very successfully as governess to three families, then spent every penny of her savings on going as a

'Private Student' to Bishop Otter College, Chichester. The Principal, Miss Trevor, recognizing her qualities recommended her when asked to advise on someone to start a small new High School for Girls at Farnworth, the Lancashire cotton-factory town. After some years of extremely hard, but successful work there, in depressing surroundings, she applied for and, as we know, obtained the headship of St. Margaret's, still at the early age of 32. It is interesting to realize, looking back over 90 years, that throughout her time and from the very start, she had always worn a lace cap which, added to her prematurely white hair and the later handicap of severe arthritis, gave the impression of a much older woman. She was only 53 at her retirement. So passed a much revered figure in the history of the School and one who went far, in the words of an obituary, to fulfil in her life's work a favourite verse from the Bible: 'So (s)he fed them with a faithful and true heart; and ruled them prudently with all (her) power'.

CHAPTER VII

THE NINETEEN-THIRTIES

THE first decade after the Great War was survived with greater success at the School than some might have imagined possible. There had been much social unrest culminating in the General Strike of 1926; the once down-trodden worker continually made fresh demands, even if many of them were to be resisted for another few years. Severe trade depression set in, producing, at its worst, 3,000,000 unemployed amongst whom were thousands of young men of the middle classes. Once more, there was a great 'run-down' of the Royal Navy with reduced recruiting, and pressure upon officers to retire early. While many of these factors might have added to RNS problems, there could be no doubt that the School and all it stood for was needed as much – if not more so – than in earlier years.

Though never without some financial anxiety they had managed to expand throughout the 1920s and the vision and enterprise behind it had been that of Miss Chaplin who had, indeed, proved to be a most able and inspiring 'Skipper'. She must also have possessed diplomacy and powers of persuasion to have carried the Committee with her on the many innovations which she put through, some of which would have seemed contrary to tradition. Those, however, who had contacts with other comparable schools would have realised that the changes were very much in the spirit of the times.

The year 1930 produced good results, with a much treasured credit balance of no less than £1309! There were some special items in this including an increase in donations of £556 but they were doing well all-round, with 141 boarders and 44 day girls, the numbers were a record and there was a long waiting list. The customary, sad note of the 'fatherless' stood at 53 indicating, yet again, the unique value of the work of the School.

The educational attainments were also excellent, with 26 sitting for the General Schools of whom 23 were awarded certificates including 13 exemptions from Matric. One girl had a place at St. Hugh's, Oxford while another went so far as to gain entrance for *both* Girton and Newnham. At a humbler level the London University Extension Registrar who inspected the School during the Summer made this impressive comment:

'It is difficult to speak sufficiently highly of the work in Latin. Each of the forms did excellent work . . . there were no disheartened failures. The whole subject is full of promise and some good scholars should be forthcoming. Corrections were beautifully done, and seemed like a breath of fresh air, bracing but not withering'. This was a fine tribute to the Classics mistress and to the response of her pupils. Plainly the increase of fun and games at St. Margaret's was in no possible sense at the expense of serious work.

The music – from the days of 24 hands performing upon 12 pianos simultaneously! – had always been a feature and it showed up well in 1930 with the examination of the Associated Board of the Royal Academy and the Royal College of Music in which 32 of the 34 candidates obtained certificates and the overall report stated that 'the music throughout the School is at a high standard'.

To accommodate all those wishing to attend when the Duchess of York, then a young mother of princesses, came to distribute the prizes, the spacious York House at Twickenham was hired for the day; this visit proved to be the forerunner to Her Royal Highness accepting the Presidency of the School in the following year, after the death of Admiral Sir Hedworth Meux.

A valuable eye-opener to many of the seniors would have been the visit organized for them to the famous St. Pancras House Improvement work at Somers Town, near Euston Station. The work inspired by a High Church clergyman, Father Jellicoe, was then a brilliant piece of pioneering under which the public subscribed to a very low interest loan to enable slum dwellings to be replaced by attractive modern flats (*not* high rise, in those days), and others to be re-conditioned. The girls were able to see both kinds as well as some of the original homes. The Day Nursery, a comparatively new concept in 1930, also much impressed them. All this type of work has long since been overtaken by the State and Local Authorities but it was a classic piece of benevolent private experiment in its day and it continues still. For St. Margaret's to go there showed a proper awareness of the needs of others less fortunate than themselves.

The exact titles of the School are a little confusing, as shown by its records, in those years: throughout the 1920s and up to 1951 the official Reports adhere to the style adopted when the 'female' was dropped in the 1890s, viz. *Royal School for Naval and Marine Officers' Daughters,* then with 1953 it became *Royal School for Daughters of Officers of the Royal Navy and Royal Marines.* Meanwhile, back in the 1920s, the magazine title was changed from the time honoured 'Victory' to *The Royal Naval School Magazine* thus introducing the simple form by which the School is most widely known to-day – 'females' or 'daughters' being taking for granted, it would appear. However, the magazine, at the start of this period, had become a fine substantial production of 64 pages, exceeding the pre-war ones, with very full accounts of all activities, in and out of School, special articles by the girls (including Samuel Pepys on *his* visit to St. Margaret's and its pretty 'wenches'), and pages of news about Old Girls.

The ups and downs of the 1930 cricket season are entertaining: RNS beaten by Cobham Ladies (surely a much older team?) 201 to 25, then they proceed to demolish Norland Place School 103 to 29. Altogether it was a good season with three matches out of five won and the fourth a draw very much in the favour of RNS.

In the early 1930s the Magazine also gave spirited accounts of the splendid and imaginative Entertainments put on by the various 'Houses'. Each one had its 'Day' in the course of the year which culminated in the evening Entertainment held in the Hall. One House did '*Lord Richard in the Pantry*' a very popular comedy of the time; another produced some form of *tableaux vivants* to represent famous paintings such as *The Death of Nelson, When did You Last See Your Father..* and the boy Handel playing the harpsichord in the dead of night – complete, of course, with night shirt. A third House of dreadful young ladies (Nelson) produced a *Fact Test* – presumably an early form of 'Master Mind' – at which ' it is to be regretted that in this the Staff did not do as well as was to be expected of them'!

In 1931 came the familiar problem of financial deficit once more, due to the curious fact that the numbers dropped temporarily and, at the same time there was an undue proportion of girls who had been accepted at the lower scales. Of all the boarders only ten were at full fees and it was reckoned that altogether there were 133 pupils at reduced fees. It had been the proud tradition hitherto that suitable girls should be admitted regardless of the amount their parents could afford to pay and subscribers were once more reminded that this practice could not be maintained unless more money came in. Few 'private' schools have much cash to spare but the RNS had a perpetual tightrope act to perform in maintaining its good standing while fulfilling its semi-charitable obligations, including the Royal Patriotic Fund beneficiaries paying their £12 per annum.

Incidentally there was an interesting change at this time with the admission of six Middlesex County Scholars among the 42 day girls, a move which could benefit both sides and which extended the opportunities of a Public School to those whose circumstances would not otherwise have made it possible. In this the RNS appeared to anticipate the recommendations of the Fleming Report of 1944 which became the basis of the famous Butler Education Act.

The proximity of the Thames, beautiful as it could be, continued to cause anxiety since the flooding of 1927. The sum of £750 had been received from the London County Council as a contribution towards the upkeep of the river wall and that had been set aside in the Maintenance Fund. In view of the age of the buildings it seemed certain that other heavy repairs would have to be tackled in the visible future. A few years later, however, the river troubles were unexpectedly lifted from them. The Heston and Isleworth Council, the School's Local Authority, in order to widen the path between St. Margaret's and the river, obtained a compulsory purchase order on a strip of their garden. An 'equitable' price of £640 was offered and, as part of the deal, the Council undertook all future responsibility for the upkeep of the river wall.

In 1933 came again the surprise resignation of their Headmistress; much admired, successful and assumed to be remaining for many more years, Miss Chaplin (affectionately known, also, to girls of the period as 'Charlie') announced that she had accepted the Headship of the North Foreland School and would leave at the end of the Summer Term. In her thirteen years she had accomplished an enormous amount for the School and the news was received by most people with shocked incredulity. A forthright letter to 'My Dear Old Girls' which she published in the Magazine said, in part,

'Judging by letters which I have received from a great many Old Girls and Parents I was considered a fixture here, and indeed there were times when I thought so myself, but I have three big reasons for making a change (you will not be told them so do not ask), and I am sure I am right in my decision.

'Let me tell you at once I do not like leaving RNS. One does not give the freshest and most enthusiastic years of one's professional life to one place, continually planning and building up, without gaining a very deep love for it. You, too, will know how attached one becomes to this place, especially the old house, and to the garden with its trees and views of the river; how the routine becomes a part of oneself; but what you cannot know, in as large a measure as I can, is the personal attachment to the members of a large family, mistresses, girls, old girls, servants, and animals.

'Some people have said, ". . . RNS will never be the same to me . . . this will be the last time I shall come for an Old Girls' Day". Now I hope that sentiment is only a pretty way of saying "I am sorry you are leaving", and no more than that; it certainly must not mean more. A School, especially an old School like this, is not dependent upon one Head Mistress. . . .'

That letter embodied something of the *credo* of a very fine Head and one who had achieved a tremendous advance for the School between its 80th and 90th years.

In a moving article for the Magazine, under the simple title *Vale*! Miss Mowat, the Second Mistress 1926–1932, wrote:

'Vision, Courage and Energy: these are the characteristics of Miss Chaplin, to which the Board of Education's Inspectors attributed the phenomenal growth and development of the School during the first six years of her Headship. Would that all official pronouncements could hit the nail so unerringly on the head!

'Vision showed Miss Chaplin the School as it might be; and to-day, with its numbers doubled, its acreage and buildings almost trebled, with modern laboratories and really good playing fields, the RNS is the fulfilment of her vision.

'To translate vision into reality, without the possibility of having success guaranteed beforehand, calls for real courage. Success is always taken for granted: no one comments on it; but failure always reaps bitter criticism. Most people, unless pressed by necessity, are content to play for safety, and to take the unenterprising path. Not so Miss Chaplin. The opportunity to take over the House and grounds of the Gordon Estate came at the critical moment, and the scheme of expansion was launched. The enterprise was at once successful, and when the Junior House had been established for a few years, the Committee purchased Ormonde Lodge to add still further to the possibilities of the School.

'Besides courage, however, the more practical virtue of energy was required if the School was to reap the full benefit of all its new amenities. This energy, and boundless enthusiasm for the best in all things, Miss Chaplin brought to the completion of the task. She was successful in inspiring in all those who were privileged to be her co-workers, something of her own zeal, and in the School itself, a new pride born of achievement was added to the old pride of tradition. The standard attained in work and the yearly number of girls who went on to the Universities was steadily raised during Miss Chaplin's time, and there could have been no more fitting crown for the advances of the period than the success of Joyce Townend in winning an Open Scholarship. It was doubly gratifying that the Scholarship was awarded for Natural Science, Miss Chaplin's subject, and at RHC, her own College.

'It is quite impossible for one person to give a picture of Miss Chaplin, for to different people she had different things to give, and it is not too much to say that no one who went to her in difficulty, worry or perplexity went away feeling that her problem was not understood, or that it was too little to be given consideration.

'One often hears people say, speaking of their old schools, "Oh, Miss X—— wouldn't remember me. I was never a success at school".

'But this was never the case at the Royal Naval School. Indeed, I think it was probably just those people who were not what one would pick out as the "successes", who best learned to know Miss Chaplin. The girls whose lives went easily on never needed her help and advice, and thus missed something of the best that School life had to give them.

'Miss Chaplin taught everybody in the School the value and beauty of the lovely old buildings and gardens. The decoration of the School was always, by her wish, kept in harmony with the austere yet gracious lines of the Senior House. There were never any fussy details, and even the youngest people in the School learned from the start to follow out her principles in their form rooms. There are many people in the world to-day who learned the canons of good taste at the Naval School, from example rather than from precept.

'The members of the Staff, no less than the girls, always knew that in difficulty they were sure of sound and understanding advice from their Head Mistress, and I know that often we must have trespassed sorely on her busy timetable. The Staff who lived at the Senior House always felt sorry for those who did not, as the latter were inevitably cut off from the social intercourse at meals which so often made Staff supper a stimulating end to the day.

'Well, she has left the School, and now we may look forward to seeing North Foreland following where the Naval School has already gone. To its members we wish the success and happiness that Miss Chaplin will take with her, and to Miss Chaplin we give what she knows is hers already – our love.'

Miss Chaplin continued her successful career but she is reported to have said, years later, that she regretted ever having left RNS.

Again the Committee was fortunate in its applicants and wise in its choice. The new Head who took up her duties in the autumn of 1933 and who was also to exercise considerable influence over the next 27 years was Miss H. M. Oakley-Hill, an Oxford graduate, who came from another famous school, Wycombe Abbey. While the Committee's Annual Report at the end of her first year vouchsafed no more than that under her 'the standard of Scholarship and the tone of the School are being fully maintained' her arrival marked the beginning of another new stage of development and it was Miss Oakley-Hill who was to shoulder with great courage and energy the tremendous responsibilities and extra burdens arising from the Second World War.

Many years later Miss Oakley-Hill referred modestly to her first few years as a time of 'quiet progress'. There was no major building undertaken then, but she very quickly made her presence felt, and in ways which must have inspired confidence.

The first Magazine to appear after her arrival contained a brief Editorial which was no doubt characteristic of her firmness and clarity of mind. After more than 40 years it still deserves recall:

Omnia mutantur, nihil interit

'Ovid, thus epigrammatically, expresses a law of the universe from which we claim no exemption.

'To the many, as yet unknown to me, who will read the School news this year, I offer this reflection, that they may know that the School they have loved is merely passing, in its integrity, through another stage in its evolution.

'To its past members it calls for continued interest; to its present members for energy and selfless service, and to the future it looks with hope and confidence, remembering that "Except the Lord build the house their labour is but lost that build it".'

One of her early innovations was to end the separation of Seniors and Juniors – apart from Hood House, and to bring together all the girls from age eleven upwards. This brought the School into line with most other Public Schools and gave scope for some responsibility to more girls. At the same time there were two new Houses Hawke and Rodney so that there were five Houses in all. By an ingenious system the Houses, which were in fact no more than groups of girls each made up of a complete age 'spread', rotated between the two main buildings Kilmorey (formerly Senior House) and Gordon (formerly Junior House). This was probably because the accommodation in Gordon was a good deal more comfortable and it had therefore to be taken in turns. Also in the general re-arrangement it was found possible to produce a Sitting-room for each House. This must have been a tremendous – and most welcome – boon. Until then there had been only the form-rooms in which the leisure time could be spent and there they had to sit at the same old desks which they occupied at class in the daytime. Photographs indicate a quite reasonable standard of comfort: gas fires in each room, a large rug on the floor, two or three easy chairs, a couch, curtains and a standard lamp – it is very doubtful how many of their public school brothers had advanced to that level at the time.

Another change of the new Head was the inclusion of her Speech Day Report in the Magazine – an invaluable innovation for the historian; and one which provides a useful survey of School events and progress year by year.

At the end of her first year in July 1934 Miss Oakley-Hill made as her first point, reference to the resignation of Miss Chaplin, emphasising the results of her work – 'the School as it is now – a place of great charm, with a wonderfully smooth organization, a fine tone, and a good educational standing. This has been passed on to me as a great structure which can well stand developments, while retaining its own character, and that character is essentially the work of Miss Chaplin'. These were generous words and wholly deserved but spoken with sincerity from one who herself had the highest professional standards.

Besides an excellent crop of exam results several interesting new features were reported; six girls successful in the Junior Housecraft Examinations of the National Council for Domestic Studies, the Historical Association visited

St. Paul's Cathedral, the Temple Church and the Mint and had a debate – bless them! – on the question 'of an Irish Republic'. Parties of girls went also to the Tower, to *The Merchant of Venice,* to a printing works, to various educational lectures at Burlington House *and,* as formerly, to the Army and Navy Rugger Match at Twickenham. (For this, the Magazine informed us that the Head Girl wrote specially to the Captain of the Navy team to assure him of their utmost loyalty despite the *red* berets which were then the School's standard head-gear!) There was also a full quota of House entertainments including *The Yeoman of the Guard.*

The new Head's Report ended with remarks which appear still most apposite: '. . . Technical requirements are becoming more exacting every year – and at the same time the whole trend of modern life is towards shorter hours of work and longer hours of leisure. There is a great danger that these hours of leisure may be frittered away in useless or even harmful ways, and it is surely one of the most important functions of a school to give girls opportunities for making good use of leisure time'.

Re-organization of the time-table shortened by one year the period before taking the School Certificate and it was urged that every girl should have at least one more year at school after it. That would give her a time when she could gain a new sense of responsibility, when intellectual growth is rapid and she could learn the habit of forming balanced and reasoned opinions. Secondly, a wider curriculum for the School Certificate was offered so that a girl could take as many subjects as she was capable of taking, and thirdly, there was the greater leisure time with a greater number of occupations to choose from. It was hoped that senior girls would make the time an opportunity to read widely and to think deeply. 'After all', she said, 'the ultimate aim of education should be to produce what Coleridge calls "thinking souls" and I interpret this most apt phrase to mean "people who can think clearly and form sound judgements because their standard of values is spiritual rather than material". I am convinced that it is on such people that the peace and progress of the world must in future depend'.

At the end of the new Headmistress's first year a very pleasant note of welcome was struck by the Head Girl, P. Owen, when she wrote 'This year, with its demands for fresh effort, has been one of great adventure in the history of the School, and Miss Oakley-Hill, with her sympathetic and generous understanding of each one of us, and her vision of an ideal School, has already won our complete confidence.

'We fully appreciate the changes she has brought about, and, in spite of our naval conservatism, are determined to make the School the success for which her leadership calls'.

There seems no doubt whatever that the new Leader showed her promise at a very early stage and it was quickly fulfilled in the tremendous tests which awaited the School during the ensuing twenty years.

To turn from an important personality back to School events, there had been a curiously worded compliment from the Inspectors in 1933 when they stated that the work in English 'was so good that it deserves the severest criticism'.

They went on to say that the teaching in the Upper Forms had been so excellent that no fault could be found with it. 'Not only have the brighter pupils been stimulated to original thought, but the weaker have been encouraged and all have been disciplined to hard work. Classes were very large and naturally uneven in consequence, but in none of them was a single instance of carelessness or indifference.' Just about every subject came out well, the only note of doubt crept in with Chemistry where the work was found uneven, but here there was soon to be improvement in the laboratories which doubtless helped in the future.

With their strange fluctuations of fortune, although the School was apparently advancing on all fronts there came a sudden dip in numbers in 1934, with only 118 boarders. This was remedied with a rise to 130 again in the following year but the drop brought a more than usual deficit in the accounts. At that time too, they were still burdened by the obligation to take ten or so boarders at only £12 per annum for the Royal Patriotic Fund.

In the circumstances there was little to spare for improvements so in July 1935 a garden Fête was organized, every House worked hard at the production of articles for sale and Lady Goodenough opened it with an eloquent appeal for funds. Best of all she set a magnificent example by going round all the stalls and buying left and right. At the end of it the Houses were able to give new curtains for the Chapel vestry and the organ, and they went on to provide £50 for the installation of an electric blower.

That was quite an innovation in those days: most small organs obtained their supply of 'wind' from the action of a large wooden lever worked up and down, by hand, in a pumping motion. Miss Margaret Holbrook recalls that: 'The Boot-boy who used to blow the organ, also hovered downstairs on the first of the month in order to be kissed by the first one to meet him with a cry of "Hares and Rabbits"! This boy, one Sunday smoked by the organ pump during the sermon and we were thrilled to see smoke coming out of the organ stops, then the organist – a rather fierce lady whose pupils said she rapped knuckles when wrong notes were played – slipped from her seat and disappeared. We could almost hear the subsequent box on the ear!'

From Miss Holbrook one also has a reminder that when the Junior House was broken up and the two new Houses formed, Hawke and Rodney, there was a certain amount of heart-burning, 'however, stiff upper lips prevailed and we settled down to the School's last seven years in the gracious buildings and lovely grounds on Thames-side'.

From the same source also, we have an amusing picture of Hood House, the home of the younger girls, under its House Mistress Mrs. H. R. Harris, who took great care to see that her charges were well turned out. In the mornings they were brought over to the main building Kilmorey and were lined up 'outside the Boot-Passage (the cloakroom) and there she personally wielded a shoe-brush in case any had not been adequately dealt with before. Clean they must be for prayers, and the culprit dealt with later! . . . Hood were a self-contained unit. They had hymn singing every Sunday evening (a happy feature of many a family early in the century), Mrs. H. playing away with gusto. I lived in Hood House – as a teacher – for a time and at night would watch Mrs. Harris entranced. She would sit in the Staff Room by the fire apparently absorbed in knitting or reading, then suddenly she would put it down and hurry upstairs, she had heard someone get out of bed, and she bounded up to deal with the offender – and she was no chicken either!' Thus were the youngest of the 'young ladies' supervised and cared for.

At that time the grounds were well looked after by a Head Gardener, Dear, and his squad of helpers would sweep the great lawns clear of leaves, with military precision. What upset Mr. Dear most of all, a few years later, was the German bomb which destroyed his best and most cherished apple tree in the kitchen garden of Gordon House. At the same time when, as is well known, the School had to leave St. Margaret's, Kew Gardens took a cutting from their Judas tree, cherished it for four years and later sent it to them at Haslemere where it has continued to flourish.

Having anticipated events slightly it is appropriate to mention one which made its mark in the late 1930s. During supper one night the parent of a day girl telephoned the School to ask if they had seen an amazing display of the Northern Lights – the Aurora Borealis – blazing across the river. Immediately the School was summoned from the dining room (from a more substantial last meal, it would seem, than in earlier years) and everyone was out on the lawn to watch the lovely – and to most, quite unusual – sight. Miss Oakley-Hill is on record as having said to the Staff, 'This bodes no good'! War was not then many years ahead.

Besides that Fête which had brought in a useful sum – and to which many parents had contributed articles for sale – there was an excellent Masque of English Literature in December 1934. A daring Magazine Editor had invited Miss Mowat to review it for them, she who had been the principal heroine behind the very successful Pageant of Education in 1927. The opening of her review struck a particularly interesting note:

'I had almost said that we were in a state of pleasurable anticipation waiting for the curtain to rise, but here, right at the start, was a startling innovation. No curtains – just a delightfully restful background of silky fawn colour.

"What? No curtains?" quoth I, "they can't possibly do without curtains".

"Can't they?" retorted a *very* new Old Girl from the row behind and Experience felt rather dashed. But what *could* be done without the venerable curtains whose charitable folds had covered a multitude of expedients, if nothing worse? Let me say that the lighting effects which superseded the curtains were the making of the whole Pageant because they allowed it to be seen as a Pageant should be seen, in a motion unbroken by the mechanical device of raising and lowering a curtain. Apart from this, by the sheer beauty of many of the effects, their use added greatly to the aesthetic satisfaction of the production as a whole. . . . When it was over and the crowds had dispersed, I went, cap in hand to Miss Oakley-Hill to ask permission to stay and see it all over again at the evening performance.' So it was good to know that besides their increasing number of alternative activities the School and its Staff had lost none of its enthusiasm and ability for the Big Production. And it was done on what might be regarded as an early form of Open Stage. Incidentally, with the aid of a certain Mr. Holbrook, they learnt quite a lot about lighting and were proud to be able to 'talk proper theatre electricians' shop, all about "perches "and "floods".'

Grenville House presented extracts from *Midsummer's Night's Dream* 'in a natural setting or, in plain words, on the rockery'. Rodney gave a Fancy Dress Dance in the garden, the VI forms went to *King Lear* in London and the Historical Society went to *Queen of Scots* at the New Theatre, accompanied by their handkerchiefs! Drake won a very amusing Inter-House Swimming Competition at Hounslow Baths, Nelson did *Quality Street*. There seems 'no end to it' as one turns the pages of the Magazine in those years and one rejoices at the interest and excitement which must have been engendered for those girls, in a school life so very different from that known to some of their mothers.

A final period touch of 1934 was the entirely new experience of 'listening-in' to a Royal Wedding broadcast, that of Princess Marina to the Duke of Kent (father of the present Duke). The ceremony 'was excellently received by the wireless. This set is sometimes temperamental but patriotism evidently lurks within its complicated bosom'.

With all these diversions there was also no slackening in work: 21 School Certificates obtained by 23 candidates and Mathematics, Chemistry and Botany all feature in the Distinctions obtained. In pressing the value of the extra year, after the School Certificate, Miss Oakley-Hill made the point that it gave, among other advantages the chance to develop a greater familiarity with English Literature. She went on to state a Great Truth: 'The English language can be the most lucid or the most obscure means of expression, and skill in its use is both a high art and an accomplishment of immense practical value. It is well worth while to strive for a good English style ... and this can only be done by wide and careful reading and by a determination never to be satisfied with a slipshod phrase nor a sentence, the meaning of which is open to doubt'.

Wise words, and needed more than ever to-day.

A school history should not lean too heavily upon the *obiter dicta* of headmistresses but one more extract from that same Report is most apposite:

'A boarding school is a miniature world. In it, as in the outer world, freedom can only exist when it is controlled and dedicated to the general good. Rules, like laws, are merely the restrictions of the individual necessary to the good of the whole, and she who so far attains to self-mastery and a sense of the general good as to be able to live in harmony and order ... has gone far towards fitting herself for the wider community of the world, and in so doing has taken one step towards the ultimate problem of humanity. ... As long as restriction of individual desire is looked upon as a grievance there will be conflict. ...'

Less has been recorded here of the religious side of the School life than was mentioned earlier. The death of the Rev. C. P. Wix, however, their Chaplain from 1917–1924, reminds one that amidst the altogether greater number of pre-occupations in the twentieth century there was no neglect of the Founder's direction that the daughters of necessitous Naval and Marine Officers should have bestowed upon them 'a good, virtuous and religious education in conformity with the Church of England'. Besides the care taken to improve the Chapel itself, there were, of course, the regular Sunday services and preparation for Confirmation, the service for the latter being taken, usually, by the Bishop of Kensington. Mr. Wix had been particularly thorough in his preparation of candidates and his wife used to have the girls to tea afterwards. He himself had successfully instituted a Sung Eucharist at the School which was greatly appreciated and he was plainly much in the tradition of a number of kindly and hard-working clergymen who took the religious life of the school under their care.

In 1935 another full programme of outside events was enjoyed, the then famous Military Tattoo at Aldershot being one, while a Summer Open Day embraced all manner of sports and side-shows, including a Parents' Cricket Match wherein 'fathers demonstrated how it should be played by soundly beating their daughters'. (So they jolly well should, one is inclined to comment, but maybe the fathers had to bowl underarm or play lefthanded!) The School Calendar, as recorded in the Magazine, ended on a light-hearted note for the Autumn Term in 1935. 'Nov. 6. A great day. No Work. This was to celebrate the wedding of Lady Alice Montagu-Scott and the Duke of Gloucester. Dec. 3. Another great day. Mumps victorious. Exeunt Omnes.'

The Official view as expressed in the Report for that year, stated that they much regretted that they were compelled, on medical advice, to close the School early for the Christmas Holidays and open it late for the Easter Term on account of the mumps epidemic. This was done to ensure a sufficient quarantine period between the closing and the re-opening. For the prize-giving in November they had refrained from having the usual distinguished visitor to present them as it was considered undesirable to expose them to infection. Still, this remained one of the very few occasions when the term dates could not be strictly adhered to.

In fact, the girls were back at School in time to attend, on January 26, the Lying-in-State of King George V in Westminster Hall, and so take their place among the hundreds of thousands of his subjects to be deeply moved by the simple splendour of that scene: the coffin resting alone on the high catafalque in the dim Hall and the magnificent jewels of the Imperial crown reflecting the candle light, in stabs of brilliant colour, as one filed slowly past.

The report on the School's music for 1935, by Victor Booth, Fellow of the Royal Academy of Music was encouraging in that the Choir was Commended for a programme showing a marvellous choice of variety and beauty but 'possibly a little exacting. . . . I cannot conceive how it was possible to accomplish so much in so short a time'. With the Orchestra he had the greatest regard for what had been done with so little material and hoped that some would take up woodwind, adding that 'the joy of team work has to be experienced to be appreciated'. It reminds us first, that the School's music continued to flourish and also the limitations in days before the Dolmetsch family had popularised the recorder and produced it cheaply, so giving to thousands of children the chance to try their skill at a wind instrument without parents having to embark upon the expense of flute or oboe (with no certainty that it would be used for very long).

An unusual outside examiner was a Miss Partridge from Wycombe Abbey, doubtless a former colleague of Miss Oakley-Hill, who came to judge the Inter-House Gym. Competition. She was presumably one of those highly professional instructresses of the day who wore the short navy-blue tunic with its square neck velvet-trimmed above a white, long-sleeved blouse, black stockings and gym shoes (the author at the age of six was much in awe of one such lady, and thrilled by any word of praise from her). Miss Partridge had higher standards than St. Margaret's, as no doubt the Head was well aware, and she showed ways in which the House Teams lacked smartness and precision. One would like to think that the daughters of sailors and marines did not need to be told twice! The inimitable Arthur Marshall might have had his fun over the gym. mistresses:

Hands on your hips girls, stiffen the upper lips girls,
March with your heads held high!

was one of his immortal songs of the 1930s, but they were fine women who accomplished a great deal for the physical education of girls enabling many of them to grow up fitter and stronger than earlier generations.

Already the Headmistress had cast her mind forward to 1940 which would be their Centenary Year and the School was warned that it was not too soon to begin to plan for appropriate celebrations . . . none could then have imagined the enormous changes which would mark that year. Certainly the next four years were full and successful though, perhaps, there were fewer dramatic changes than have been noted in the early part of the decade.

With the continual increase in School activities running costs showed a tendency to rise though this was partly offset by some useful additions to the annual donations. King George's Fund for Sailors now produced an annual £1000 and the Lords Commissioners of Admiralty £480, yet in 1938 they faced a deficit of £1100. This necessitated a rise of 5 % in the fees and at last there was some relief in the heavy obligation to the Royal Patriotic Fund, to maintain five pupils in the School at their very much reduced rate. This, it will be remembered, was in consideration of the £5000 given in 1856 to complete the purchase of St. Margaret's. Extremely valuable as that had been at the time, the terms had become somewhat onerous.

In 1937, a brilliant former pupil Joyce Townend, became one of only two women to obtain First Class Honours for her B.Sc. in Botany – this from the Royal Holloway College – another had Second Class Honours in English and there were other Honours in Modern History; academic standards were being more than maintained. Bridget Evans made history for the School as the first to take a full Classical Course and to gain entrance to Newnham, in Classics, being specially commended, while, on an entirely original tack, Jean Bruce gained a scholarship at the Reville School of Fashion for a series of original fashion plates. This must, at the time, have seemed a wholly revolutionary development for an RNS girl but it is all proof of the wide variety of opportunities offered.

An innovation also introduced was a course in shorthand and typing for those who stayed on for another year after taking their School Certificate. As the Headmistress pointed out – exactly in line with the advice of so many employers – those two skills can be of great value to a girl, whatever career she may finally adopt. Certainly they have been the means of *entry* for able girls into thousands upon thousands of business, and other occupations, though subsequently they have risen far beyond typewriter and shorthand book. It must also have been one of the skills least affected, in terms of employment, by the vicissitudes of the Economy over the past forty years. Though the courses lapsed after a time it is interesting to find that these two subjects have been re-introduced in recent years.

In that same Report Miss Oakley-Hill made special mention of her Staff saying that they were a most loyal body of people 'willing at all times to spend themselves for the sake of the School; and here I think is my opportunity to pay tribute not only to the Staff but also to last year's Sixth Form, who proved themselves Prefects of unfailing readiness to lead and to serve'. This was the first public commendation of the Prefects and stands as another example of the way in which the School was developing. A further change was the, then striking, decision to abolish all House and Form marks replacing them with a new system of Grades.

So, in all its different departments, the School moved on in good order towards the end of that last decade of the inter-war years. It was not to be found wanting in either the quality of its Leadership or the spirit of the girls themselves as they faced the trials of the Nineteen Forties.

CHAPTER VIII

THE SECOND WORLD WAR

THERE were few people in positions of reponsibility who were taken wholly by surprise when war was declared in 1939. It was natural therefore that men so well informed of events as the Committee of the RNS should have had long discussions, in July and August of that year, about the future of the School in the event of war. At length it was decided to carry on at St. Margaret's and in the remarkable chain of events which followed, including their Providential escape from injury when bombs fell, it was doubtless the right decision at the time. Miss Oakley-Hill and Miss Hussey were much concerned with all the practical arrangements and the following pages are based upon notes made many years later by the Headmistress herself.

Many parents, when notified that the School would remain near London, decided to withdraw their daughters and quickly the number of boarders fell to about 80 so that, when an appeal went out for extra beds for hospitals – in anticipation of thousands of air-raid casualties – the School was able to send about forty. Meanwhile, with the start of the Autumn term in that September work continued normally and with the usual quota of Day girls.

The Head herself had unexpectedly to face an additional burden: the former Bursar, Paymaster Captain Smith, left and his successor did not prove equal to the complexity of school accounts with the result that Miss Oakley-Hill was obliged to act as her own Bursar and shoulder a totally unexpected burden of extra work for the duration of the war. Granted that she doubtless had assistance with the clerical side of the work, it was distinctly a feat to have acted, in a sense, as the business manager as well as Headmistress throughout six years of constant change and inevitable anxiety.

Hood House was closed in that first term and Kilmorey partially so, thus the reduced running costs brought a welcome improvement in the accounts which had showed losses during the previous two years. As the Autumn of the 'phoney war' passed without air-raids over England it was confidently felt that they had been right not to leave the London area – a view shared by scores of other City-based organizations at the time, though another nine months put a very different complexion upon it all. However, more girls came back in January 1940 and Kilmorey House was re-opened. Then again, by the summer, when sporadic daylight raids over London began, more girls were withdrawn and with the reduced number it was decided to have all meals served in Gordon House, while the basement of Kilmorey was equipped as a shelter. Gordon was unsuitable for this because, had the river wall been badly damaged, the basement of that House would have been flooded.

Games and normal lessons were frequently interrupted by air-raid warnings during late June and July and girls were – at that early stage – frequently found looking out of the basement windows to watch the aerial 'dog fights' over London between RAF and Luftwaffe planes. Against continual blue skies of that memorable summer the terrible business of brave young men fighting to the death, thousands of feet up, was made to appear deceptively beautiful by the great white vapour trails which often followed machines as they banked and looped, manoeuvring for position to destroy the enemy.

By contrast, little more than three months earlier, the Headmistress had seen the School celebrate its Centenary. April 2nd, the day of the month when the first Committee had met in 1840 at that 'Thatched House Tavern', St. James's Street, had found her sitting 'on the balcony, with a heron floating overhead, and the river running dark green and cool just beyond the wall, in the lovely peace of these buildings and grounds which have stood quietly watching so much history go by. It is hard to realize that not far from here valiant men are giving their lives once more to save all that has eternal value for mankind. . . . If the Youth of England has to-day a freedom undreamt of in 1840, it also has demands on its courage, its self-control and its faith which have never been equalled . . .'

The private celebrations had been held on the actual Day – a whole holiday without bell or rules and, after a short Service of Thanksgiving, just enough occupation to prevent boredom. The Acting Chairman Miss Blanche Egerton and Lady Goodenough, whose husband Admiral Sir William Goodenough was a Vice-President, had skilfully collaborated in the pooling of their own (and doubtless some of their friends') rations to produce a magnificent cake. Decked out in the School colours it was in every way worthy of the occasion and must have added much to a happy day – especially to young ladies who were already feeling the effects of sweet rationing.

The Centenary Day ended in the evening with another splendid series of scenes, organized by Miss Hussey and the Historical Society (History *was* her subject and she must have been a marvellous teacher of it). They evoked the Story of the School from the awe-inspiring entry of the first Lady Governess, Miss Clifton, through the heroic performances on the massed pianos, the mechanical repetitions of historical facts from a textbook – 'theirs not to reason why, hers not to make reply!' – and so on to the Kilmorey of 1940 with its bare-legged high-spirited activities.

Before returning to the upheavals of War it is worth recalling how deeply impressed Miss Oakley-Hill was, just before its outbreak to have ample evidence of the strength of affection which bound successive generations to the School. She could report letters from Old Girls from India and from China announcing the birth of daughters and asking that their names should be entered at once on the waiting list. Another, on reading the Magazine, felt so homesick for the place that she felt she must 'write and talk about it'. The dignity of it, not least of the buildings and the grounds, was something which impressed both pupils and visiting parents. This sense of loyalty towards the RNS was something which endured and proved of great value in the years ahead.

With the start of the Autumn term of 1940 came the real test for St. Margaret's as for everyone in the South-East of England. The parents of girls who lived in London and Portsmouth allowed them to remain at the School when it became clear that those two areas were targets for enemy action. The 70 boarders and staff all slept in the Kilmorey basement as originally planned.

During those September days of constant distractions with the continual need to 'take cover' an amazing feat of concentration was shown by one girl, Isobel Stoddart, who had to work much of the time lying on her basement bed amidst all the noise, yet she gained her Oxford entrance with the choice of both Lady Margaret Hall and St. Hugh's College.

Soon after the beginning of that term the voice of that British traitor, known as 'Lord Haw-Haw', was heard on the School radio set saying: 'Gairmany calling, Gairmany calling, we are sorry to have to bomb the Naval School – so upsetting for the fathers at sea'. That voice of enemy propaganda was rightly laughed off by most people, as a rule, and much of it was sheer invention but this was no empty threat and the School faced it with the utmost courage.

One night during the holidays when Miss Oakley-Hill herself was on watch, on the top floor, with her maid (the redoubtable Irish Mollie Moody whom we met during the First War) a flare floated down over the grounds, 'Ah me goodness' said Mollie, 'the mune's coming down' . . . It evidently showed the enemy what they wanted because thereafter bombs seemed to come nearer every night, one landing on Canada House part of which was badly damaged. The situation was potentially terrifying but they held on until a few nights later when again the Headmistress was on duty with one of her staff, Miss Loveland. They heard the rush of a falling bomb just as they came to the foot of the main stairs and as they crouched down all the front doors and windows were blown in with a tremendous crash. They dashed down to the basement where the girls were and shouted, 'Quick, under your beds!' and they did it in one movement.

The main building stood the shock that time but the bomb had broken all the front windows of Kilmorey and the Domestic Science Room as well as tearing a branch from the big cedar tree.

The next morning they acted with great dispatch. All parents were wired or telephoned to collect their girls from the School as there was no chance of continuing normal routine and plainly they were under systematic attack. The Headmistress phoned the Chaplain of the Fleet for details of any large house the Admiralty might still have on its list and she was given the names and addresses of some, including Trafalgar House which had generously been offered by Lord Nelson.

She and Miss Hussey drove down to Salisbury Plain to look at it and one other house but they both proved quite unsuitable and were too remote. The latter point was serious as petrol was already rationed and soon became virtually unobtainable except for essential purposes. For most people domestic pleasure motoring ceased to exist for much of the war. Shortly after this, however, the Admiralty released its option on Verdley Place, just south of Fernhurst, near Haslemere, which proved capable of taking seventy girls and some staff.

Directly Miss Egerton and Admiral Goodenough had inspected it the Committee agreed that it should be leased at £1092 per annum. A large country house of the sort usually described as 'rambling' with numerous odd landings and staircases, it was far from ideal, in fact, but it provided a temporary home and avoided what might otherwise have been a serious dissolution of the whole

School. Carter Paterson had been offered the wartime use of Gordon House after one of their London buildings was destroyed, and being on the spot at once undertook the whole move of the School into the country. In the words of Miss Oakley-Hill 'they were marvellously helpful in every way'. Only essential furniture could be taken, the rest was stored in the School chapel – one can just imagine the task of sorting it and making the decisions. However, Verdley Place was somehow made ready, and the parents were all notified again and 48 boarders reassembled. That move was Providential.

As soon as they had settled in, the Head, Miss Hussey and Miss Holbrook drove up to Twickenham to collect their own things. Almost as soon as they arrived an evening raid began. Fire bombs fell on the Kilmorey roof and, with the utmost pluck, the ladies rushed up to try to extinguish them. They were joined by official Air Raid Wardens but the flames quickly spread and the Wardens sent them down where they spent the rest of the night in a small shelter with Mrs. Dear, the gardener's wife. After Kilmorey was well ablaze it was hit by a very large bomb which undermined the foundations and burst all the water mains. Thereafter it was a ruin. The Report of that year later recorded of those three Mistresses that 'Their courage was beyond all praise'. It was unquestionably their part of England's Finest Hour.

After two uncomfortable winters at Fernhurst there came a near-miraculous deliverance. One evening in the Spring term of 1942, when a Sixth form play was in progress, O.-H. was called to the phone. It was from a Miss Smith who was about to close her own school near Hindhead. She said: 'I understand you are not altogether happy in your present conditions. We should like to sell our house here – could you come and see it?'

O.-H. took the first of her many hundreds of drives up the long, narrow, deep-cut Farnham Lane and spent some time looking over Stoatley Hall which she described as 'a large house in a splendid position, which could hold a hundred girls and it had a large gymnasium, a beautiful swimming bath and lovely grounds with a superb view down to the sea coast nearly 30 miles away'.

She continued, 'I rang up Miss Egerton and told her about it, and it was arranged that she and Admiral Goodenough should go with me and see it. We did so and it was decided almost at once that the School would buy it'.

Ten years later Miss Hussey wrote for the Magazine her own most vivid account of those war-time migrations of 1940-42: 'It was a grim calendar: September 28th, incendiaries in the School grounds; September 29th, Kilmorey and Gordon damaged by blast; September 30th, term suspended; November 27th, RNS re-assembled at Verdley Place; November 29th, Kilmorey destroyed by high explosives. Set against the backcloth of European history these intimate items in a School Calendar may seem unimportant threads in a flaming tapestry, but they were sombre threads with an ugly twist for us, and they were woven closely into our lives; though since then they have straightened out and the tints have brightened.

'For those who lived through the events five entries in a Calendar are sufficient to recall all too vividly the nightmares of those eighteen months when

a. New Kilmorey block opened in 1952.

b. Art Room.

c. Domestic Science in action.

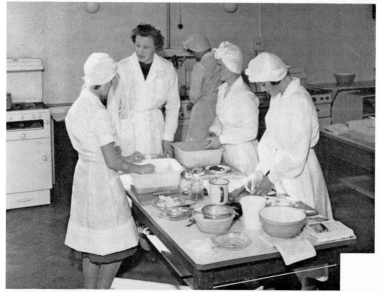

a. Aerial view
   of Stoatley Hall.

Games in the 1960s:

b. Net ball.

c. Cheerful Lacrosse
   team.

b

c

we did our best to run a Public School in furnished lodgings, but the majority of those in the School now were either still in the cradle or, at most toddling optimists in evacuated nurseries, so they know little of it. I shall always remember Miss Loveland's cryptic comment as she stepped out of Miss Macdonald's Hillman Minx on to the front drive at Verdley: "Just like the Sleeping Beauty's palace," she said – and so it was.

'Miss Oakley-Hill's heart-breaking hunt for evacuation quarters, during those six weeks from September to November, had taken her far afield, through several counties, and in and out of a good many of the stately and the not-so-stately homes of England. Rumour ran rife meanwhile among the Staff who were running a temporary School for a few marooned boarders and a number of day girls – spasmodic lessons punctuated by sojourns in the shelters listening to the guns. "We were going to Devon!" "No, that's off, it's Cornwall, probably near Truro." "And what about that place up near Morecambe?" "Oh, another school is going there. She has gone to Salisbury to-day." "We may get a place in Hampshire." "What, not really?" "No, it's Sussex, I tell you." "Yes, positively. Verdley Place." And actually, yes it was, and the agreement was signed on November 6th. And this was the "Sleeping Beauty's Palace"!

'Your car nosed its way up a winding drive thick with overhanging rhododendrons; you penetrated the house through double doors, the outer one doubly-locked; you found yourself in a panelled hall and in rooms where an Edwardian hey-day stood still and remembered its past magnificence. Now, tired hydrangea thrust through shutters into the lower rooms, clematis clung to the upper storeys, wisteria climbed across the roof tiles and ivy crawled into a nursery where toys which children had played with in the nineties lay disconsolate, the fireguard graced an empty grate, and the cuckoo clock was silent.

'Here, then, we established ourselves. Sometimes we were very near to tears, but sometimes how we laughed! The Sixth Form were installed in the Drawing Room, where Queen Anne cabriolets and gilded chairs and Georgian fire-screens looked askance at desks and uprights. Indeed everywhere School furniture was wedged between untouchable antiques, or, anyway, pseudo-antiques!

'The time-table of these days was an interesting document; it had to be annotated and it read something like this: Lower Sixth French (in the Coach House); Lower Fifth History (in the Garage Attic); Upper Fourth English (in the Housekeeper's Sitting-room); Form III (in the Servants' Hall); and I can picture Miss Pritchard and Crystal Hancock doing Higher Chemistry in a dim cubby hole where the boot boy used in palmier days to polish baronial, even royal, footgear! The two grand pianos in the Drawing Room were kept locked, so piano practice went on in peculiar places like the Nursery Alcove and the China Pantry and the Butler's Recess. I used to wonder why the butler had a recess and what he did in it. Anyway there we put a piano and there the Parnells, the Bennetts and the Severs practised their Polonaises and their Moments Musicaux. The bedrooms, too, had none of their present nautical smack. You slept in "Lavender", or "Small White" or "Great North Spare" or "House-maids Three" or "Sir Felix", and here you were in exalted proximity, for the Headmistress occupied the "Dressing-room-through-the-Red-Baize-Door"!

'The shutters were certainly an advantage in World War II, but they were by no means Nazi-proof, and Operation "Curtains" was one of the major enterprises in the Migration to Verdley. Anyway there were no shutters where they would have been most help – at the oddly placed oriels high in the turrets – so an energetic Live-wire in a green overall took charge, aided and abetted by a Tower of Strength in the person of John Smith. She was to be seen perched precariously at the top of rickety ladders for days on end and she was christened "Lady Black-Out", but her other name was Holbrook.

'Another live wire was Miss Macdonald, who did Trojan work in every department of Verdley. She was Secretary-cum-Chauffeur-cum-House Mistress, and, indeed, first-to-hand in any emergency. It was she, with Miss Loveland, who organised the removal from Kilmorey to Fernhurst from the Twickenham end.

'The Kitchen Front was an important Sector. Anyone in the vicinity in the early months at Verdley was usually able to appreciate the difficulties from the audible imprecations, over the giant oil stoves and the vast range, uttered persuasively by the Cook of the moment; then there were the intervals of domestic infelicity in between the Cook who had departed because she could not cope and the Cook who was coming and who we hoped would prove she could; and at these times any Teaching Staff who happened to have a free period (gratuitous term!) cast aside their academic gowns and plunged into the kitchen to lend a hand and help make fish pie or mince perhaps for ninety. "Perhaps" was indeed the word, as few of us had much idea of large scale quantities, so we did multiplication sums on scraps of kitchen paper with sometimes staggering results; I remember one day making chocolate sauce with Mademoiselle Favry, and between us we produced a positive Nile Delta of it, of peculiarly muddy aspect, but the School disposed of it philosophically, recognising it as just another example of the luck of the Navy.

'Perhaps I have said enough to make you appreciate the occasion on February 21st, 1942, when Miss Oakley-Hill announced to a thunder-struck assembly that we were to move to Stoatley in April. Usually the School stands in serried rows and listens apparently unmoved to official pronouncements. But not that day! Miss Oakley-Hill described the joys in store. "Fourteen bathrooms", said she. Shouts of delight from the School, who had queued for eighteen months for tepid ablutions in "Sir Felix's Bathroom", or the Night Nursery. "Sixteen others", said she. Shrieks of appreciation at this brilliantly discreet description of plumbing marvels rare at Verdley. "AND A SWIMMING BATH", said she. The School roared its applause, and we did no more Preparation that day. So next the move.

'If the Migration to Verdley had been fantastic that to Stoatley was stupendous. Fourteen pantechnicons from Twickenham and eight from Verdley wound up Farnham Lane, the first arriving on April 14th, and a squad of Staff worked like furies in the process of disgorging and distributing. And I must record here that two stalwart Old Girls, Jill Wyatt and Rosamund Hastie Smith appeared on the scene to render yeoman service in the enterprise. I remember our first luncheon in Stoatley. We sat on the floor of the present Lower Sixth

Form Room and enjoyed tinned salmon and black coffee. Fish knives and forks? Certainly not. "Pass the Headmistress a penknife, and where is Our Spoon?"

'The School assembled here on May 8th. RNS owes a great deal to the two Head Girls of those Migrations, Isobel Stoddart and Daphne Parnell, who, supported by a band of Seniors, kept alive innumerable Kilmorey traditions.'

Stoatley Hall itself, well-built mainly in stone in 1902, had been originally the property of a wealthy City man and with the very handsome and expensive panelling of its hall and staircase was similar in some respects to a number of other dwellings in the neighbourhood. Mostly they belong to the turn of the century period when the Hindhead area had become popular with people seeking natural beauty not too far from London; but for the individual owner such great houses could be kept up only in the age of negligible taxation and unlimited cheap domestic labour. Even so, to reach them from a railway station before the advent of mass produced cars was quite an undertaking. An interesting sidelight upon the 'servicing' of Stoatley Hall in its pre-1914 days is the recollection of one Haslemere man, Mr. Fred Bowden, who as a boy helped his father in the regular delivery of coal to it. Two tons at a time they carried up, in the standard four-wheel coal cart of those days, behind two great cart horses in tandem. Three-quarters of an hour it took from St. Christopher's Green, including rest pauses for the horses and they could not be stopped on the steeper sections – any other traffic had to give way to them! – another world, but it serves to remind one of some of the reasons why such dwellings were not in great demand by 1942. An organisation such as a school, with its priority claims for heating, transport, etc. was the only likely occupant, and they obtained it for about £10,000.

The estate agents' survey indicated much that was in bad order, 'soiled' generally worn, badly tarnished' etc. were phrases that occurred frequently and it is clear that Miss Smith had not been prospering with her school but the potential for the RNS was tremendous. For a start there were 19 bedrooms, at least 3 fine reception rooms plus billiard room, flower room, staff room, cottage, 'loose box' and the curious feature of 'engine room for deep well pump.' Much re-decoration had to be done, in due course, before the house was in a really fit state for the growing School but enough was accomplished to make it habitable between the date of possession April 8th and the start of the summer term in 1942. There were no Easter holidays for O.H. and her staff that year.

Actually it was found necessary to limit numbers to 84 boarders at the start but a year after, the adjoining house High Rough was leased, and a few years later, purchased outright. That extra space enabled numbers to rise to 120 which was important as there was then a long waiting list.

The precise financial arrangements which enabled these large property transactions to take place are too complicated to detail here and at first sight it is well-nigh incredible that an 'institution' which had experienced continual problems in meeting its expenses from year to year, should be able to put its hands upon £32,000, the approximate cost of all the land and buildings acquired at Haslemere between 1942 and 1944.

The starting point had obviously been the enthusiasm and belief in the project by the Headmistress, Miss Egerton and Admiral Goodenough. King George's Fund for Sailors and the then Board of Education were first consulted. The former was donating a regular £1500 a year, and it was naturally of the utmost importance that the Board should approve in view of the financial assistance likely, or hoped for, at some stage. An increase in the School fees coupled with a drop in expenditure because of the negligible amount of repairs and renewals possible in wartime had improved the cash position. They could anticipate, one day, getting a useful sum in compensation for the Twickenham land and buildings (in fact they were compulsorily purchased on reasonable terms by the Middlesex County Council, at the end of the War). They also realised part of their invested funds which had been slowly built up over a hundred years, and then there was a magnificent windfall of £10,000 from the Johannesburg Navy Week. The whole operation was well in the tradition shown earlier with the St. Margaret's expansions and, again, as in the time of Miss Chaplin, it originated with the vision and enterprise of the Headmistress.

With all these stirring events there was nonetheless a creditable exam record kept up though the numbers taking their School Certificate naturally declined with the reduction of the pupils in the School. However, the proportion of passes was good: 19 out of 21 reported in 1940 and 10 out of 11 in the following year, 7 gaining exemption from the Matric. Two girls also obtained Higher Certificates, one gaining her exemption from Intermediate B.Sc. and – very much a sign of the times – a Government Scholarship for University Training in Radiolocation (that invention which played so great a part in the aerial defence of Britain from 1940 onwards).

In these years, and through to the 1950s, Miss Oakley-Hill and Miss Hussey, as Second Mistress, combined as a most effective pair for the running of the School, their different characteristics successfully complementing each other. The former, her pale blue eyes below the fair, then white, hair coolly appraised people and situations. Seeming to many perhaps not very approachable, she certainly carried a tremendous load of administrative work throughout the war period and like any good head of an organization she knew how to delegate. In Eileen Hussey there was the ideal second-in-command, though curiously, in that strictly Anglican atmosphere, she was a devout Catholic (who did not, however, permit her beliefs to bias the teaching of her subject which was History). Miss Hussey was a considerable personality in her own right: it was said that she possessed 'a terrific voice' which, while it could swiftly put a malefactor in her place, was also an instrument which continually spread enthusiasm and encouragement. Behind the scenes, she had been reponsible for much of the success of the famous *Pageant of Education* which she and Miss Mowat had put on together in 1927. She was a great driving force during the early years at Haslemere; she was herself eminently approachable and there were few girls who would hesitate to go to her when in difficulty of any kind. Some have described her as the supreme 'buffer' and executive for the Headmistress and there can be no doubt that over more than thirty years Miss Hussey, who was deeply attached to RNS and all it stood for, made a very great contribution to its well being at many levels.

Under strict war-time petrol restrictions, the School could not come down into Haslemere very frequently by motor transport, but groups of the more senior girls soon became a familiar and welcome sight. They quite often made the brisk walk down to St. Christopher's Church and back, about three miles in all, climbing up the 400' on the return. At times also, some came across by footpath to reach the Parish Church, St. Bartholomew's. The strict standards of their Headmistress, with her emphasis on Dignity, ensured that whether or not (under clothes rationing) many of the uniforms were second-hand, an RNS contingent of Sailors' Daughters must look always well turned out. The navy blue suit with white blouse, the traditional black tippet and sailor hat were unquestionably 'fetching' to many a male who saw them as a charming form of WRNS in miniature. Incidentally that famous 'tippet' had been introduced by Miss Chaplin as a mark of respect at the time of the Court Mourning for Queen Alexandra. The girls took to it, the tippet was seen as a neat addition to their uniform and so it has remained for over 50 years.

There were some who regretted that the School should have settled so far away from the centre of Haslemere, thus being unable to take as much part in the local life as one might wish, on the other hand no buildings and land of suitable size were readily available at the time and had they existed the cost would have been prohibitive. In the event, the rapid increase in the use of cars within a comparatively short time after the war, largely eliminated this problem. It is interesting to see that in 1975 the Summer Term Calendar announced no fewer than 20 important events, of one kind and another, in which the RNS participated *away* from the School. The image of the 'Nunnery on the Hill' has long since been dispelled!

The 'One Hundred and Fourth Annual Report' of the Committee in 1944 sadly noted the sudden death of Miss Blanche Egerton, in 1943, so soon after she had played her vital part in supporting the move to Stoatley Hall. The School had been the major interest of her life for some 30 years; and she had devoted a great deal of time and energy to it; she had been one of the Vice-Patronesses as well as having become a very senior member of the Committee and on the outbreak of war in 1939 she had become Acting-Chairman as the then Chairman, Admiral Sir Herbert Meade-Featherstonehaugh, had to return to Naval duties.

A small increase in the teaching staff was made in that year to deal with the larger number, then up to 120, but they achieved a useful surplus of over £1600 *after* the investment of £1000 for the amortisation of the cost of the buildings. This was one more of the consequences of the impossibility of spending more than the barest minimum upon repairs and decoration during the War: the cash position, at least, was comfortable and there was opportunity to accumulate funds for the heavy expenditure which must come later.

In that year of 1944 which brought the wonderful news of the successful Normandy landings and the invasion of Europe, there were many more dangers still to be faced by the fathers and brothers of RNS girls but the tide of War had clearly turned. Plans could be thought about for the visible future when England would be at peace. Apart from a few 'Buzz Bombs' (the V-1 German rockets) which drifted badly off course in July, the Haslemere area had nothing more to fear from air-attack.

The chief event of that year in School life was the re-institution of Hood House, the original of which had been closed at St. Margaret's on the outbreak of war. The name was given to High Rough which then included the Third and Second forms. Financially, the main event was the astonishing surplus of £3587 income over expenditure, after allocating £1000 for amortisation of the cost of the new buildings as usual. Part was due to most generous donations in which King George's Fund for Sailors continued to feature largely. This was also the year of the £10,000 from Johannesburg.

Examination results were more than satisfactory with 16 School Certificates gained out of 17 candidates, 7 gaining Matric exemption and there were also 3 Higher School Certificates.

Unhappily there came at this time, and so soon after Miss Egerton, the death of another valiant supporter, Admiral Sir William Goodenough. He too had been a member of the Committee for very many years and had given generously of his time and money to the School.

So, the RNS came safely through to the end of six years of Hitler's War with 1945 showing still further progress. The year drew to a close with a formal Speech Day when prizes were given away, most fittingly, by the Hon. Lady Goodenough.

CHAPTER IX

MID-CENTURY ADVANCE

At the start of the 1947 Report which covered the first complete year since the end of hostilities, a warm tribute was paid to the Headmistress and her Staff for the magnificent work they had accomplished during the previous six years. Some such acknowledgement was normally made right at the end of the Report and its promotion in the order was significant and well deserved. To have kept the School on an even keel through those years was a very great – and at times no doubt a wearisome – achievement and one of the sort all too readily taken for granted unless things go badly wrong. To be able to record that the health of the School had remained good also meant that skill and ingenuity had been exercised by the catering staff in producing adequate meals from the monotonous rations of the time and that matrons and school doctors had been ever alert to any signs of illness.

It should be added here that in her first post-war Speech Day Report, actually reprinted in the 1947 Magazine O.H. had gone out of her way to emphasise the special part played by leading members of her Staff. She said:

'Now I ask any of you who have moved during the war to imagine the task involved in the double move of the School, and the organization necessary for expansion. In this great task, I have been able to rely unfailingly upon those members of the Staff who have been with us through thick and thin, from Kilmorey onwards, Miss Hussey, Miss Holbrook, Miss Loveland and Miss Lupton, and especially Miss Hussey, our Second Mistress, whose intimate knowledge of historical characters and events of every shape and size, is only equalled by her ability to organize removals; and to Miss Holbrook, who has adapted her Art to everything from war to peace, or may I say, from blackout to bunting. I can never repay the debt I owe to them during these years of transition.' (And one can bet that it was all done willingly without a penny of overtime or special allowances of any kind.) It was a generous tribute and, one does not doubt, that it was extremely well deserved.

O.H. had ever a fine turn of phrase and a stirring message for her girls at the conclusion of her Reports. On this very special occasion she ended:

. . . 'give of yourselves whole-heartedly, in understanding, in sympathy, in work and play; and remember too, that the staff who teach you are not concerned merely to stuff you with facts. They are interested in you as people, and they expect you to react. They can take you to the water and say "Drink, puppy, drink", but will you drink? Will you react as real people to the real people teaching you?

'I say to you Seniors, realise, here and now, your seniority. . . . Take your full share in your homes. Give to your parents real companionship and understanding of their problems. Don't go on taking all that is done for you for granted. Don't be guests in life taking all the care and love as if it cost nothing,

. . . the more you will give of yourself, the more you will enrich your personality
. . . .'

The immediate Post War period brought a deep sense of anti-climax, disappointment and frustration to many people. That civilians were no longer in danger from air-raids of any kind and that their loved ones had been restored to them from active service, was soon forgotten in the realisation that all forms of rationing, including petrol, were to continue; that Great Britain, despite victory, was a poorer country and still quite unable to return at once to its former standard of living in for example, food, clothing, furnishings and foreign travel. This all led to much disgruntlement and irritation in many quarters but it is greatly to the credit of the RNS and its staff that there appears no word, in the records, of any despondency there during those years. On the contrary there was soon evidence of new vitality and growth.

A smaller Prize Giving had taken place in December 1944 when Lady Tait had officiated and that had at once shown up the need for a proper Assembly Hall. The fine, panelled entrance hall at Stoatley was not lacking in dignity and was splendid for a smaller gathering but the entertainment of any substantial number involved endless movement of furniture and general upheaval. Plans were afoot for extensions but the time was not then ripe.

Meanwhile, it is good to see that 1945 was the last year in which O.H. was officially described as 'Headmistress and Bursar', thereafter Miss Alderson, succeeded by others, relieved her of one part of her workload, the Bursarship. Running costs increased steeply. The end of the wartime Lease-Lend arrangement with the United States was a serious factor in adding to our food costs while salaries and wages rose to keep pace with inflation (though its rate at that time was trifling compared to that of 1975). As if these were not enough, it was found that the near-fifty year old gas main was in need of complete renewal and opportunity was taken to employ more efficient gas heating. Thus, although fees had risen it became difficult to cover costs and the School was more dependent upon the various donations which fortunately tended to increase at that time.

Academic work was proceeding satisfactorily and the music was obviously flourishing with 23 girls passing their various grades in the Associated Board of the Royal School of Music. This was something to be enjoyed without hindrance and with little dependence upon rationed commodities 'in short supply' – to quote the contemporary jargon for the word 'scarce'. The simple beauty of the School choir broadcast of Hymns in the BBC Children's Hour Programme on November 17th 1946 is still remembered by some of us. It was an excellent example of their choral training.

In the following year the number of boarders had been squeezed up to 140 and there was a long waiting list. The Committee noted many 'expressions of appreciation of the work and training of the School and an understanding that it was of great benefit to the Navy'. Slightly curious wording, perhaps, but clear evidence that they were pleased with the achievements at Stoatley Hall.

Late in 1947 RNS received another of the charming gestures to reaffirm their Royal Patronage when a substantial part of the wedding cake of our present Queen, then Princess Elizabeth, and the Duke of Edinburgh was sent to them. The Princess had then accepted the Presidency of the School.

In the following year there fell one more of those blows inevitable with ageing property which has had little spent upon it for several years: the roof and coping of Stoatley Hall were found to be in bad condition and £4000 was needed at once for its repair to fit it for the further battering of south-westerly gales in an exposed position. New kitchen equipment had also to be paid for at the same period so that the usual £1000 could not be put to the amortisation fund in that year. Nevertheless, the additional pupils accommodated brought in welcome extra fees so that overall there was only a small deficit. Donations and sundry legacies continued still, despite the changed financial circumstances of so many people.

It is a matter of historic interest that within three years of the end of the War the great War Damage Claim for the loss of the St. Margaret's property was agreed at the sum of £29,363 and *with interest* at $2\frac{1}{2}\%$ from November 1940 – the latter an extremely useful sum in itself. With the Building Fund which had been steadily accumulating and investments which stood at over £100,000 it was then possible to consider seriously the further necessary expansion.

The nearby Thursley House had been acquired earlier to give accommodation for 10 more girls bringing the total up to 130 boarders and also enabling the Domestic Science department to be re-established. The latter was provided in a good room with full equipment for cookery also for needlework, and there was a large Common Room for the girls which had been badly needed.

Miss Oakley-Hill had already made her plans for this moment and by 1950 came forward with details for the new building which is now known as Kilmorey. Her ingenious layout of Assembly Hall and stage at one end with the Chapel Chancel at the other, containing altar, choir stalls and organ, all of which can be entirely screened off, was an inspiration. On the floor above were classrooms and more bedrooms. It was at once realised that the extra revenue from fees which this increased number of girls would bring in would be more than enough to compensate for the loss of interest on the capital expended and it appears that the Committee quickly agreed to proceed. There was also the urgent need to increase their numbers to make the running of the School more economic under the pressure of higher costs. There was to be accommodation for 40 more girls which would bring up the total number of boarders to 180 and the state of the waiting list fully justified such provision.

No new building could be done, then, without Government Licence but with the backing of the Ministry of Education, and doubtless the appropriate word put in by the Admiralty, the required licences were forthcoming so that by the date of the Speech Day, October 20 in 1951, the Ceremony of laying the Foundation Stone was carried out by Instructor Rear-Admiral Sir Arthur Hall (whose wide contacts and powers of diplomacy had been invaluable in tackling the various government departments). A Service of Dedication and Blessing of the Stone was conducted by the Rector of Haslemere, the Rev. Gordon Shelford, in the presence of the whole School and of a large number of parents.

These building matters have carried us ahead of our main story which had not advanced beyond the year 1950. The events of that year were well described in the Magazine for 1951 which, itself presented an interesting New Look. Though printed in smaller type and upon thinner paper than the pre-war issues – in accordance with the current 'Austerity' measures – it ran to 70 pages and contained 13 pages of advertisements. This latter had been the suggestion of Miss Chaplin, the much admired 'Skipper' of the 1920s who continued as Vice-President of the Old Girls' Association, and the £50 net profit from this had been just enough to balance the Magazine account. With its useful reminders of local hotels, car hire firms, estate agents, etc. – not forgetting Peter Jones 'Official Outfitters to the RNS' – the advertisement section was a valuable feature.

Quite excellent photographs of the handsome south front of Stoatley Hall with its beautiful wooded background, the unquestionably 'cosy' look of the gabled two-storey High Rough and, well caught by Miss P. Ermen of Upper VI, a snap of that utterly freak, heavy snow storm of April 26th 1950. It showed the amazing beauty of the snow covered grounds in the bright Spring sunshine.

Another illustration portrayed what was most rightly termed a red-letter day, the Prize-giving of that year when the chief guest was Earl Mountbatten of Burma. He is shown, looking marvellously youthful, in the splendour of his heavily decorated admiral's uniform, and judging by the smiles of all around – including the Headmistress – he has just produced an amusing 'crack' for the delighted young recipient of a prize. Well might Admiral Sir Harold Walker, who took the Chair, remind the School and its visitors of the astonishing career of Lord Mountbatten: a Naval Captain at the start of the War rising swiftly to have supreme control Combined Operations with the responsibility for planning the Normandy landings, and then to become Supreme Allied Commander of the newly formed South East Asia Command where he commanded the campaign which successfully drove the Japanese out of Burma. In 1947 he took on the most difficult task of the last Viceroy of India to negotiate the Transfer of Power. His success is measured by the fact that the Indians asked him to remain on as their first constitutional Governor-General, and eventually he opted to return to the Navy as the Flag Officer Commanding the First Cruiser Squadron in the Mediterranean, First Sea Lord and finally Chief of the Defence Staff. (In 1955 the RNS was further honoured to have him as their President.)

Academic successes were well kept up with entrances gained for Lady Margaret Hall and to Newnham while fresh ground was broken by Bridget Jepson who was the last link with Kilmorey at Twickenham and having gained her exemption from the 1st M.B. had become a medical student at St. Bartholomew's Hospital; there were also 100 per cent successes in both General and Higher School Certificate Examinations.

The School Calendar for 1950–51 was, if anything, fuller than in St. Margaret's days. A cinema projector had been acquired and three or four good films – (some 'improving' and others just good fun) – could now be shown each term. The Choir took part in an Albert Hall performance of Bach's Mass in B Minor; Farnborough Air Display was visited by some and the usual quota of House plays was given, O.H. and Miss Hussey making a point of always attending the latter. They must have enjoyed Grenville's performance of *Emma* wherein a young Female named Carol Irving, playing Mr. Woodhouse, 'never forgot that her back was bent and her "legs-not-as-good-as-they-were", nor that draughts were perpetually lurking to annoy her'!

The joy of their own swimming bath now made it possible to hold a regular House Swimming Competition. A very nice touch, also, in a year when an exceptionally early Easter fell within the Spring term, was that on the Easter Sunday all the School Services were conducted by the Chaplain of the Fleet. It is rare that a 'padre' of the Services fails to make a strong appeal to young people.

After nearly ten years in Haslemere a good fixture list with other schools had been built up in tennis, lacrosse and netball, extending as far afield as Portsmouth, Reading, Ascot and Guildford, so there was even less justification for the earlier suggestions that the RNS kept itself 'too much to itself' at the top of the hill. Politically too, they did not stand aloof from the General Election of 1950, as both Labour and Conservative Candidates for the area came to address the girls and to answer questions.

A feature of the Magazine, from its first publication in 1905, had always been a good coverage of Old Girls' activities and in the early post-war period this went from strength to strength. The section arranged in four Groups, according to a girl's period at the School, extending from 20 to no less than 36 pages with the issue of 1952. It meant a great deal of work for the Editors but was very worthwhile and must surely indicate an exceptional degree of interest and loyalty towards the Old School. (One is quite unaware of any male establishment taking so much trouble in the matter!) Understandably, after the world-wide movements of the War period, there were few parts of the globe in which RNS girls were not then to be found and one of them contributed a perceptive article 'South Africa With the Lid Off' revealing the difficult problem of the coloured population, well before the subject had become a newspaper commonplace.

Mrs. Fowler, the former Miss Helen Stone (Principal 1904-1914), like two of her predecessors, lived to a considerable age, dying very peacefully near Winchester in February 1952. She was much beloved and the last Magazine reference to her had been a note of thanks for the great number of cards she had received from former pupils at Christmas. A very interesting obituary appeared in *The Times* and summed up her unique place in the history of the RNS. ' . . . . She was one of many Old Cheltonians trained by Miss Beale, who became Headmistresses of important girls' schools. She was appointed to the Royal Naval School at a time of transition, and during the ten years of her tenure of the post she grafted a more liberal régime and curriculum on to the somewhat rigorous discipline which had been the tradition of the School. All who came under her influence remember her gracious charm and the high ideals of duty and thoroughness which she inspired.' This was high praise from such a quarter, and well deserved for her who had so successfully performed the task of infusing fresh life into an essentially Victorian 'Institution' to bring it triumphantly into the twentieth century.

A final glance at the Magazine for 1952 shows that there was plenty of imagination and writing ability in RNS at the time: no fewer than ten pages are occupied with excellent descriptions of *Our Visit to a Glass Works* and to *The Dolmetsch Workshops,* an extremely funny piece *Skeleton Crew* on those 45 who stayed behind to the last week of the Autumn term when the rest had gone home to avoid a mumps quarantine, also three sensitive essays and some quite good little poems.

The Report and the Magazine of the following year gave wonderful evidence of material progress. The building programme for the new Kilmorey block, begun in 1951 was fulfilled within twelve months so that it came into use in September 1952 thus making possible the essential expansion of numbers up to 180 boarders. A very attractive Prize Day photo of that year showed Admiral of the Fleet Lord Fraser of North Cape in uniform presenting books to a very pretty Head Girl, Jane Kelly, while her Headmistress in gown and hood keeps an eye on the proceedings. A sequel to this was that the Admiral subsequently arranged for Miss Kelly to attend the next State Opening of Parliament.

Earlier there was obviously great interest and fun for the girls while the new building was in construction – even if it meant some anxiety, at times, for their safety. They saw it all rise from mere trenches in the ground, and like all of us when unaccustomed to building work, thought, 'But it all looks so small' .... and then as the roof goes on, 'But it all looks so dark!' An extract from an article about it by Elizabeth Studdert shows how instructive the experience was for them: ' .... on the bare concrete floor of the hall lay the huge girders destined to become the joists of the ceiling. We used to climb over them and wonder how they were to be lifted up .... We had stared at the vast hole where the boiler was to go, and the week-end that it was put in was a landmark .... we examined the knobs and gauges with great interest. Half way up the stairs, where the Staff flat is now, we watched the room growing and it was fascinating to see the little holes in the wall turning into lighting and heating appliances .... then to see the whole expanse of the bedroom floor without its partitions.

'After the summer holidays a transformation had taken place. The hall, which had been dark and gloomy, had become light; upstairs, evidence of the future had sprung up everywhere; beautifully appointed bathrooms, a hair washing room with rows of basins, sprayers and hair-driers and – wonder of wonders – footbaths in a little room by themselves! The bedrooms have little wash cubicles of their own and, to the relief of all heads of bedrooms, the cubicle bars are far too small for anybody to swing on them!'

The Speech Day rehearsal, it was said, 'was carried out to the accompaniment of a bulldozer which was flattening the hills and valleys of earth covered with brambles, which are now the wide flat space behind Kilmorey' but in the end all was finished on time.

It must have been a very proud day for Miss Oakley-Hill and Miss Hussey; with that new building and its equipment the School once again came right up to date, and surely ahead of many. In her speech for 1952 O.H. gave her own amusing account of the run-up: after complimenting the architect, Mr. Bostock, and the Haslemere builders Chapman, Lowry and Puttick on their good work (in particular their foreman, Mr. Wild who, in spite of the intricacies of the job never failed 'in calmness, patience or courtesy') she said that during the last few days 'a friendly battle for the possession of the Hall has been waged between the School and the painters and carpenters. On Monday, armed with 170 chairs we took it by assault, and took up our Speech Day places with bulldozer to the right of us and steam roller to the left. In the evening we retreated in good order to supper, without loss of chairs, leaving the painters in possession. On Wednesday we returned to the attack with the same chairs and some reinforcements much to the amusement of our opponents, and this time we carried even the citadel of the platform and achieved a complete rehearsal of to-day's proceedings.' (Did not Bernard Shaw say that no man is any match for a woman?)

Glancing back to the early years of the School the Headmistress recalled the lovely and gracious building which had been their home from 1857 to 1940 and announced that in memory of it the new building was to be named 'Kilmorey' – 'a name dear to generations of girls, including some who are now in this Hall as parents'. A particularly interesting summary of RNS girls' careers followed after she remarked;

'There are many "New Parents" here to-day and I think they might like to know what some of the girls who have left in the last few years are doing. Two are at Cambridge, one doing Mathematics and one History. Two are medical students, one at St. Bartholomew's and one at St. Thomas's. One is at the Middle Temple and will shortly be called to the Bar. One has just gained a degree in Science at the University of London. One is in her third year at Bedford Physical Training College. One has gained her LRAM and is teaching music. Two have trained at Art Schools; five are teaching, or training to do so; several are training as Physio- and Occupational Therapists; a number have trained as nurses at Bart's, the Middlesex and Thomas's, and at Orthopaedic Hospitals, and others have trained at Domestic Science Colleges. So you can feel that many possible careers are open to your daughters.'

It was a record of which any Head might feel proud – especially after six years of war and two removals. Also it was a remarkable fulfilment of the prophecies made by Miss Chignell in her *Victory* article, over 30 years before, after the 1914 War (see page 69), and is again a measure of the enormous progress made in the position and opportunities for women since that April day in 1840 which marked the foundation of the School.

Little mention has been made of the series of School Doctors who looked after the girls, since those serious epidemics of the last century, but RNS was never without good care in this respect. After the move from Twickenham they were fortunate to have the services of the leading man in the Haslemere partnership, then Dr. Oliver Gray. In 1952 he was specially welcomed back by O.H. in her Report, after his recent illness, and she recalled his great 'interest and

H

kindness to us ever since we first arrived at Fernhurst as refugees from a destroyed school in 1940, and we are very grateful to him for his ready help and advice at all times'. Latterly they have been well cared for over many years by Dr. R. Milton, another highly qualified Senior in the local Group Practice.

Incidentally, all these developments were taking place with the general standard of living at a level which few industrial workers would accept to-day. Television had barely re-started and was still a luxury – colour undreamt of – home central heating was very rare as was 'wall-to-wall' carpeting – pretty coloured china had been 'For Export only'; it was all plain white here, and the revolution in man-made fibres for clothing was yet to come. And though petrol was cheap enough the ownership of relatively new cars was by no means general, if one had a car at all! It is the more creditable that one finds little complaint of such 'austerities' from what may be read of the School at that time. In one of her Speech Day addresses O.H. had, however, made a reference to them when she said: ' . . . . in ordinary family life we are faced with *lack of quality* at every turn. Utility material for our clothes, shoddy in texture and in dye: utility china as ordinary as it is rare. There are many reasons for this but its effect upon the rising generation must be bad. We older people have the advantage of memories of lovely material, exquisite china, fine books – endless things upon which care had been lavished. Those who are now aged 9-15 have no memories behind rations and utility, and there is a danger that they should come to regard these things as normal and lose any real sense of quality. What is the remedy for this? My answer is, of course, Education.'

While accepting that, up to a point, shabby clothes and shabby uniform did not matter, she went on to emphasise that there came a point when they did matter, because *they have an effect on the mind.* 'To children who are always shabby, shabbiness and lack of care become engrained, and are seen in work and play. Well kept rooms, well treated furniture, well appointed tables, *well mended clothes;* these things matter now as they have not mattered before . . . . We at home and in School *must never accept the utility attitude of mind,* that lazy thought, it will do . . . . recover in yourself this sense of QUALITY. Whether sweeping a floor, 'she went on, 'polishing a table, writing an essay in faultless grammar with well formed writing, or playing a game, be satisfied with nothing less than perfection so far as it lies in your power'; it was a good message for that particular moment in our domestic history.

In 1953 there came two Royal events which touched the School; the death of Queen Mary, recorded in the Magazine by a reproduction of the historic photograph showing Her Majesty accompanied by Miss Chaplin, in gown and hood (and curiously enough, herself carrying the Queen's bouquet) at the opening of Gordon House in 1923. Then there was, of course, the Coronation of our present Queen in June of that year. The arrangements were vividly described well by 'S. Gwynn (Upper VI)' – curious how rarely contributors were allowed Christian names – and one is reminded again of 1911 'only more so'.

The start from Haslemere had to be made at 3 o'clock in the morning after a 'very sustaining breakfast', one is relieved to know. There could be no more than twenty of them accommodated and Miss Gwynn had a lucky number in 'the agonising draw'. Reaching London as dawn was breaking they had a rendezvous with other schools and cadets at Eaton Square, then, with large labels round all their necks they were 'herded like sheep into their pen' to their places on the Victorial Memorial. There they stuck it out for some ten hours, thrilled by the sights, but caught, from about midday on, by that 'terrible relentless rain, which manages to pour down one's neck and back and soak one to the skin in a matter of minutes; around one an extraordinary collection of newspaper hats and tarpaulins were erected by the crowd in a vain attempt to keep dry. We were so packed in that we could not reach our pockets to get out our bérets, and so sat with the water pouring off the brims of our panamas down the neck of some unfortunate neighbour . . . . After each shower, the Guards shook their busbies and clouds of water flew out, soaking the indignant crowd!' But at the crucial moment of the return of the crowned Queen, nothing could dim the RNS contingent:

'The great glass panels of the golden coach enabled us to see Her Majesty amazingly well. As the great roar of cheers went up we pulled our hats off and waved them as well. The Queen smiled at us and spoke to the Duke of Edinburgh at her side; he also smiled at our frenzied waving'. After having made 'a hasty check to make sure that no bodies were underfoot or lost, we then glued our eyes on to the Palace' where among the other Royalties appeared two little children 'both madly excited' – the future Prince of Wales and Princess Anne, later to be their President. So they came at last to the end of Coronation Day – 'a day which none of us who went to London will ever forget'.

In that year the official name of the School was changed to *The Royal School for the Daughters of Officers of the Royal Navy and Royal Marines*. It was also the time of the dreaded outbreaks of poliomyelitis among the young and they closed the summer term early as one girl had been affected. Providentially she made a good recovery and prompt action by the School doctors prevented a major outbreak.

By the autumn of 1954 all of the new Kilmorey Building was occupied and the Magazine showed a good photo of the Hall and its stage. It had cost £47,000 altogether but thanks to some of the major donations mentioned earlier (and the insurance payment upon the St. Margaret's buildings) they were already paying off annual instalments of the amount borrowed from the original Endowment Fund.

By skilful sleight-of-hand, without the Head's knowledge, a beautiful plaque was prepared for the wall of Kilmorey stating that it was named after their original Home beside the Thames which was destroyed by bombs in 1940 and to record the Twenty-One years of Miss Oakley-Hill's headship. The presentation was made by the Head Girl in a simple but dignified ceremony, at the end of an ordinary Morning Assembly, which came as a complete surprise to the Recipient and gave very great pleasure. In that same year the new stage was utilised to the full with a wholly outstanding production of *Richard of Bordeaux* by Miss Hussey. It received not only a full review in the Magazine by Miss Keppel-Jones but a vivid 'Impression' also, by O.H., and in a note by the Producer herself special thanks were given to Miss Holbrook for heraldry, props and make-up; to Miss Codrington for costumes, and to Miss Rawlins for head-dresses. It was another very fine piece of team-work and, sadly, the last of its kind to be directed by Eileen Hussey.

By the mid-1950s as the long reign of O.H. was drawing to its close the School continued to advance. The number reached 200 including 20 day-girls and the extra income from fees produced the first real surplus in the accounts for ten years. Allied to this, however, was the continual – though well deserved – rise in Staff salaries. The number of them was not increasing significantly but the totals for 1955 and 1956 were £13,000 and £14,000 respectively, while for 1956 it was expected to be £16,250 under the new scales. Not surprisingly fees also rose and by 1957 reached £285 p.a. but the waiting list remained healthy.

In 1955 the Chancel was added to the Hall at its east end, and the original organ from St. Margaret's installed, so that another of the building schemes was completed, helped largely by the proceeds of Chapel collections, an Old Girls' Fund and an excellent Fête held during the previous summer in which the side-show 'Dolls of All Nations' had been a great attraction. In a good year also there was a highly satisfactory Ministry of Education Report to cheer them still further.

The next year's Magazine showed the RNS thread running through the generations with an attractive photograph of 17 girls and Miss Holbrook, the very successful Art mistress, all of whom were daughters of Old Girls of the School. So time moved rapidly on to the climax of that era, the visit of Her Majesty Queen Elizabeth the Queen Mother on the Speech Day of 1958. By what was termed a 'wonderful Keith Prowse' plan, and surely a masterpiece of compression no fewer than 489 bodies were seated in the new Hall. Local Dignitaries, the Headmistress *and* the present and immediate past Head Girls were presented at the arrival, and when Her Majesty entered the Hall a posse of Juniors near the door 'won a very pleased smile from her by their well-timed curtsey.'

It must have been a proud and most happy day for many people, old and young. Her Majesty herself made a short but most effective speech. After looking back to her last visit to the School at Twickenham nearly 30 years before she said that ' . . . . it has gone forward, accepting challenges with courage and determination, and to-day it stands stronger in numbers and higher in reputation than ever before in its history . . . . The speed of life to-day and the immensities of its problems may tempt you to feel that you cannot possibly affect the issue. I do most firmly believe that this is not true. The final decision in every case, whether it is for good or evil, in great matters or small, always has and always will rest on the individual . . . . '

The thanks of the School were well expressed by the Head Girl, Jennifer Hamilton, who concluded with the words, 'We cannot expect to make full use of our opportunities without the example of others older and more experienced than ourselves. We have indeed in yourself and in Her Majesty the Queen two shining examples.'

a

b

(a) Mrs. Charlotte McClenaghan and Rear Admiral Sir John Fleming with
Princess Marina and Admiral of the Fleet, the Earl Mountbatten (1966).
(b) High Rough, the Sixth Form House.

a. Miss Diana Otter with Earl Mountbatten and General Sir Ian Riches in 1971.

b. Choir practice in the Chapel.

During these great events RNS were not neglecting their games and in one year, 1957, they did well in their tennis, profiting perhaps from the new tennis courts recently provided, and at lacrosse they won every single match. At a more mundane level it should also be mentioned that under Miss Gower the keeping of hens and pigs had prospered: fresh eggs for the girls three times a week, and pigs had passed their final examination of the Marketing Board with 3 A Grades!

Also with 1958, had come the completion of 25 years at the School for both the Headmistress and Miss Holbrook: presentations were made to both of them on Old Girls' Day and charming letters of thanks from both appeared in the next Magazine addressed to 'My dear Old Staff and Old Girls.'

In the following year came the sad death of Inst.-Rear Admiral Sir Arthur Hall who, only a year before, had presided so happily at the visit of the Queen Mother. He had given great service to the School having joined the Committee in 1941 and become Chairman two years later. The Report said of him: 'We cannot do better than quote from the Memorial Address at St. Martin-in-the-Fields:

'We thank God for a man whose service and example has uplifted all that he touched'.

Now came the inevitable announcement of the pending retirement of Miss Oakley-Hill herself and rightly did the Committee record their appreciation of 'the magnificent work she has accomplished since 1933. Accounts of the manner in which she dealt with the crisis at Twickenham in November 1940, and how she found the School at Haslemere, will appear elsewhere. Her lasting memorial is in the character, grace and education of the girls who have been under her care and guidance – even more than the buildings at Haslemere. We thank her and wish her health, happiness and long life'. They also placed on record 'appreciation of the efficient and loyal team work of Miss Hussey and the staff of all departments'.

At her last Speech Day in 1959 O.H. concluded by remarking that 'The School and I have travelled a long way together and with me two companions of 27 years, Miss Hussey and Miss Holbrook who shared with me strange days of school in a basement and sandbagged windows. . . . I can say that I have had the happiest relationships with staff and girls. I shall leave them with much sadness and with lasting gratitude for their constant loyalty and friendship. A great many hundreds of girls who have passed through the School in my time have kept in touch with me and I have been delighted to welcome their daughters as members of the School – 14 of them are here now and further applications are always coming in . . . my wish for them is that they should go out into the world with Grace of heart which they can bring to bear on every situation they may meet in life'.

On July 9th of the following year, in the presence of nearly 800 people, the retiring Headmistress was presented with a gold wrist watch from the Old Girls' Association and with a cheque by Rear-Admiral Sir Philip Clarke on behalf of the Committee. Also, from her Staff came the honour of a portrait of herself to be presented to the School and that now hangs at the top of the main staircase.

Of the many fine tributes to O.H.'s great work for the School that by Miss Holbrook, in the Magazine, emphasised three particular achievements:

'The external monuments to her foresight, drive and efficiency are here for all to see. We have a flourishing School – the School which she carried through the war years. RNS never closed down. After the bombing at Twickenham Miss Oakley-Hill hunted the countryside for a temporary home, from Castles in the North to Manors in the South. . . . There must be hundreds of "her" girls all over the world who are Doctors, Barristers, Vets, Institutional Managers, Nurses, etc. – and, yes, fine wives and mothers! . . . At all times girls and her staff knew that they could go to her for help and advice about their careers and about their troubles. Her keen brain and her great heart were always at their service.'

So passed into her well earned retirement a great and gifted Head Mistress. By a sad stroke of fate Eileen Hussey her Second Mistress and friend, with whom she had worked in perfect harmony for so long, died suddenly after an operation, in September of the same year. She had spent her entire professional life at RNS and the many references to her in this book leave no doubt of the vital part she had taken in the life, work and entertainments of the School. Besides her unfailing loyalty and support to her Head she was a great 'character' in her own right.

The departure of these two distinguished ladies within so short a time represented the turning of a most important page in the history of the School.

CHAPTER X

THE LATEST YEARS

GREAT as had been the progress of the Post War period, it was realised that, for the 1960s, the School must set a fresh course to meet the rapid changes coming upon society – economic, social and behavioural. Older people might decry them and consider that not all such changes are for the better, but a fair minded observer could not suggest that, in general, girls of the RNS are not fully the equals in character and integrity of their predecessors. In many of their achievements they are probably superior.

A deliberate change was therefore sought in the choice of Mrs. Charlotte McClenaghan, Senior English Mistress at Battle Abbey, Sussex, M.A. and Senior Moderator (First Class Hons.) and Gold Medallist of Trinity College, Dublin. Herself the mother of daughters, she was able to bring a different and more liberal outlook to bear upon the School. Inevitably there was criticism when the 'young ladies' were, for example, permitted by her to appear in public – on their exeats – in the comfort and informality of slacks (just like other girls!) but these were minor points. On more formal occasions they turned out just as smartly as ever and what really mattered was that fresh drive and energy swept through the organization. It was quickly seen that once again a good appointment had been made by the managing group, now very properly re-named, Governors.

On her first Speech Day Mrs. McClenaghan mourned the sudden death of Miss Hussey, upon whom she had relied to show her the ropes at the outset, but she at once announced that she had appointed in her place two Second Mistresses Miss Holbrook (Residential) and Mrs. Stemson (Academic), moves which proved popular and successful. The new Head stressed that 'work and scholarship are our *raison d'etre*' and RNS became one of the earliest, if not the first, School to have three Sixth Forms. They consisted of the usual two: Upper and Lower, working for 'A' levels and a 'General' Sixth doing a one year general course (now the Business Studies Course) for the less academically gifted, but who had also obtained their GCE 'O' levels.

Against this, a dance, the first of several, was actually held in Kilmorey, partly to pay back invitations accepted earlier from the male establishments ('Goodness, they're here' was the anguished cry from bedrooms as the coach arrived on the tick of 7.50 pm, 'last bits of make-up were frantically dabbed on before we dashed down to meet them') any shyness was soon overcome and an extremely good time was had, the only problem being the exceptional number of hours it seemed to take some girls to get to sleep after it all.

A good Open Day was held, partly for Old Girls, in the summer and over 600, including parents were present. From 11.30 there were displays of athletics, work done, including printing and pottery, with 'all exercise books open to inspection' – a 'Bring and Buy' which raised £170 to help the re-decoration of

House rooms – House tennis finals – and it all ended up with family picnic parties around the grounds 'just like Glyndebourne' it was said (and they *had* heard Act One of *Dido and Aeneas* rendered earlier).

In 1962 it could be reported that RNS had again 'pioneered' by creating, in High Rough, a Sixth Form House: it already had a suitable common-room and a pantry was fitted up with a gas stove where they could brew their own warm drinks and even cook their own suppers on Saturday night, as well as all meals on Sundays (if they wished, and if they had no School duties on that day). Girls were growing up more quickly and in danger of finding it increasingly irksome to remain at school long enough to secure the higher qualifications demanded of them. In Mrs. McClenaghan's words 'I feel we have got to help them meet the new situation, where possible, by relaxing school disciplines and rules formulated to deal with a less mature 16 or 17 year old'. The big increase in Sixth Form numbers was due both to the improved arrangements in High Rough and to the attraction of the new General course. The principle has been continued with complete success.

Another sure sign of progress, and well-established reputation in these years, was the continual growth in numbers. By 1963 they had reached 177 boarders and 57 day girls. Inevitably with the run-down of the Navy, the proportion of daughters-of-the-sea, was beginning to decline in relation to those of civilians. That meant, however, that there were fewer with claims for the lower rate of fees and this naturally helped the financial position. Moreover, it was clear that the RNS was attracting plenty of applications entirely on its considerable merits. It was one more great contrast with the very early 1900s when the Annual Report had constantly to remind subscribers to make more widely known the 'advantages of the Institution' because there were then several vacancies. From 1960 onwards the waiting list has normally extended for about five years ahead.

Miss Holbrook brought her long career at the School to an end by her retirement in 1964, though she did once again act as escort to a party of Sixth Formers on a Mediterranean School cruise two years later. Her Art teaching there had spanned no less than 31 years and her connection with the RNS went back several years earlier – when she had first arrived as a very small girl. Like Miss Hussey she had been a popular teacher and an invaluable support to more than one Headmistress.

So there came the great year of 1966 in which was celebrated the 125 years of the School's existence – very properly they waited until the 125th year had been accomplished. The celebrations were spread over three days, the outstanding event being the visit of H.R.H. Princess Marina, on the first day, July 8th, when all Old Girls were invited to attend. On a fine sunny afternoon 300 of them turned up including two remarkable ladies Mrs. Williams and Mrs. Gough, both of whom had left the School in 1902, in the time of Miss Leys. The two previous Headmistresses were there, Miss Chaplin and Miss Oakley-Hill, and attractively set out displays and exhibitions were on view, while music of the Royal Marine Band from Portsmouth was played – always a delightful accompaniment to an open air function.

On her arrival, Princess Marina, who had done most of the journey by helicopter, was received by Earl Mountbatten of Burma, the President of the School. Her Royal Highness was then conducted round the School and showed particular interest in a display, illustrating the making of cosmetics, in the chemistry lab, where she chose a lip-stick specially made for her colouring (there was reliable evidence that she had it in use some little time after!). The Sixth Form had the privilege of entertaining the royal visitor to tea and the photograph suggests that it was a happy affair.

On the second day, which was allocated to parents and the many friends of the School, two performances of the pageant of the School's history were needed to ensure that all guests had an opportunity to see this most attractive production. Then, on the Sunday, came what must have been a singularly fine and impressive service in Guildford Cathedral, attended by a congregation of over 1000, including some hundreds of Old Girls, besides the entire School with many parents and friends. The Chaplain of the Fleet, the Venerable Archdeacon C. Prior, CB, QHC, officiated, Miss Bostock, the principal Music Mistress was at the organ, assisted at rehearsals by one of her gifted School pupils Nicolette Eustace. Reporting upon all the celebrations later the Head expressed very special thanks to 'those whose efforts of organization were quietly and unostentatiously pursued for months beforehand' – they were well merited.

For that year also, Mrs. McClenaghan could report 100% successes in their Advanced Level results with 8 distinctions, and 78% success at Ordinary Level as proof that work was not being neglected. Athletics too, had sprung into greater prominence than the ordinary games at that stage; one girl actually reached the Semi-Finals of the 150 yards in the All England Athletic Championships.

One can only high-light a few of the interesting, and in many respects, exciting achievements of these last years. In that 126th year there were RNS girls at no fewer than ten different universities and there was a remarkable spread both of subjects and countries: one girl so far away as Wellington, NZ, and another on a special scholarship at St. Louis, USA. Some of the less usual careers being taken up were Forensic Medicine, Retail Trade with Fortnum & Mason, Display, Bi-lingual Secretarial Courses and Institutional Management. Two exceptionally able girls, Patricia Tomlins and Susan Dowling, obtained 1st Class Honours, B.Sc. (London) in, respectively, Physiology and Anatomy. Yet Mrs. McClenaghan, with her characteristic human touch, pointed out in one of her Reports, 'To those disappointed in exams I would say it is a verifiable fact that there is no exact correspondence between classification of individuals on exam results and the contribution made by them in later life'.

When, in her penultimate year, the Head referred to satisfactory results in both 'O' and 'A' levels she was generous in her praise of her . . . 'staff of high calibre – not surprising, as they are happy to come to a well-equipped school, in pleasant surroundings where classes are small and the pupils well-mannered'. In her final year Mrs. McClenaghan returned to this theme, saying that the many potential applicants for her position, whom she had shown over the School recently, had all expressed delight at the buildings, equipment and lay-out. Those were outside professional opinions from people with experience of other schools and it reflected very favourably upon the skilled and devoted work of Heads, Staff and the unfailing support of the one-time Committee, now the Governors.

Mrs. McClenaghan retired at her own wish in 1970, having accomplished exactly what she had set out to do. Great changes, to some revolutionary, had been effected but the overall results had been good and by generally accepted standards the School was prospering on the higher plateau it had reached.

Now, a firm decision was taken to select an altogether younger Headmistress. It was considered that the more rapidly maturing girls of the 1970s might be most successfully directed and guided by one not too far distant from them in age. Accordingly, Miss Diana M. Otter, who might, to some, have seemed 'very young' was appointed. She held the degrees of BA (Hons) London, AKC, Dip Ed (Oxon) and was previously Head of the History Department at the High School, Putney, one of the famous schools of the Girls' Public Day School Trust. The historian may reflect that Miss Leys, a revered and much loved Headmistress in her very different era, was almost exactly the same age, when, in 1883 she began her reign at St. Margaret's.

The events of the last five years have amply justified the Governors' choice. The School has remained full up in spite of added accommodation, with 183 boarders and 100 day girls, many of the latter being picked up daily at Haslemere Station by the School's neat navy blue bus with its red lettering.

One of Miss Otter's early appeals was to the parents of day girls to encourage them to participate as fully as possible in every side of the School's life, especially the extra mural activities. Efforts were made to ensure that no girl should ever feel at a loose end during her leisure hours: a Games Room was evolved out of some formerly unused space at Stoatley, badminton made possible in the Gym. and the Art Room was open at week-ends. The Upper V was also accorded the privilege of coffee-making in its new Common Room and by 1972 the new Head could report the 'heartening and gratifying' news that 27 out of 40 in that form had elected to stay on for VI Form work over another one or two years.

In the following year the principle of *non-teaching* Resident House Mistresses was introduced. This was partly due to the growing number of non-resident mistresses, many of them married, who wished to be away to their homes promptly at 4 p.m. each day. The system has worked well and enhances the idea of a change, for the girls, to a homely atmosphere after the more strictly disciplined day's work 'in School'.

There has been an interesting return, actually, to the system practised originally at St. Margaret's, by which each 'House' in the School now lives as an individual House, i.e. Grenville House resides at 'Thursley', Drake and Rodney Houses in two separate units at 'Stoatley' and Nelson House at 'High Rough'.

Concern for the good use of leisure was given further practical shape by the building of the new Leisure Centre beyond, and to the north of, the Music Centre in the main Stoatley Hall block. It is a light and spacious room in which a good floor for dancing and a coffee bar are prominent. The idea has proved a thoroughgoing success and has given opportunity to invite and entertain other schools there. Also there is now a new craft and needlework room which girls can use in their leisure time.

Over the years, and beginning actually in the time of Mrs. McClenaghan, there has evolved the policy to concentrate all teaching in the Kilmorey block thus reducing the amount of movement between the various rooms for each class period. With the new construction needed to meet the larger number of pupils there is now a fine block of modern classrooms grouped together. Enough has been said to demonstrate, beyond doubt, that with its present Headmistress, the School continues its vigorous growth seeking all the time to provide, at reasonable cost, the best that enlightened and responsible teaching can offer.

A request by the writer for an entirely informal meeting with some senior VI Form girls was readily granted by Miss Otter and arranged by their House Mistress Mrs. Reed. Upon a dark Friday evening the front drive of High Rough was well lit up to guide the not-so-young driver safely in. The Head Girl herself, Nichola Baxter, welcomed the visitor charmingly, relieved him of his coat and led him up to the cosy sitting room of the House Mistress where some half-dozen Young Ladies of the Upper VI were pleasantly at ease, some sitting on the floor.

Their week-end had begun, they could wear what they liked and some impressive 4-inch heels were visible on the high black boots . . . we were a gloriously long way from Hope House, Richmond Green, in 1840. After serving the coffee Mrs. Reed withdrew and the visitor, just a trifle apprehensive, was on his own – to sink or swim. He need not have worried; after a question or two, stimulating talk flowed easily and an intended three-quarters of an hour became an hour and a half. For him it was quite one of the most 'enjoyable-ever' encounters of its kind and the impressions made most strongly by these lively, intelligent and attractive girls were:

First, how glad they were to have decided to take their extra two years in the Sixth Form ('it's not until you're through your "O" levels that you begin to know what work really *is* about').

Second, the sheer interest and stimulus they found in it all.

Third, the pleasures of their form of life in High Rough, with its individual study-bedrooms, its somewhat easier routines and the satisfaction of having earned their privileges; at the same time they gladly accepted the added responsibilities of their position in a School in which they took such pride.

To the outsider it appears to be a wonderful fulfilment of the aims of two Headmistresses, at least, Mrs. McClenaghan and Miss Otter, who have striven to build up a strong 'Sixth'.

In 1976 one may feel that beyond all the good organization and the splendid surroundings there is a successful adherence to the spirit of Miss Otter's statement in the prospectus that:

'The years that a girl spends at The Royal Naval School represents a bridge between childhood and maturity. It is during this period that she must learn the art of self-discipline, controlled responsibility, and the subtle balance between freedom and order.

'Essentially the School is a community in which people can fulfil themselves and bring out their own particular talents to the best advantage. It is a community where there is a small number of accepted, essential conventions which are readily observed by every member in exchange for the growing advantages which she draws from this membership'.

At this stage it is, perhaps, appropriate to look back over the years to 1840 and to see how Admiral Williams' 'child' has been carefully nurtured to maturity. His Committee and their successors have all been surely embued with the spirit of the words traditionally used in the launching of H.M. ships – 'May God bless this ship and all who sail in her'. Equally surely their selection of Headmistresses has invariably been both wise and happy, while they have shown great wisdom in their strict adherence to the dictum that their function is 'to appoint the Headmistress and not to disappoint her'. In other words, they have consistently given successive headmistresses all possible support in their duties, while at the same time refraining from unnecessary interference.

The results speak for themselves, and it is not surprising that the RNS is confidently poised to meet whatever challenge the future may bring, greatly honoured and encouraged by the recent announcement that H.R.H. Princess Anne has graciously consented to be its President, as from January 1st, 1976, in succession to the Earl Mountbatten of Burma, to whom the well-being of the School has meant so much.

INDEX

Adam, Robert, 71
Albany, Duchess of, 48
Alexandra, Queen, 101
Anne, Princess, 9, 120

Battenburg, Admiral Prince Louis of, 58
Beale, Miss Dorothea, 15, 42, 54-5
Beth Book, The, 19, 28, 36, 38
Bowden-Smith, Admiral, 53
Brenton, Rear-Admiral Sir Jaheel, 16
Buckingham Palace, 51, 72
Buss, Miss Frances, 42

Careers of RNS girls, 62, 70, 91, 109, 114
Cavendish, Capt. Henry, 78
Chaplin, Miss A. E., 9
  appointment, 68-9
  designated 'Headmistress', 73
  achievements, 80
  resignation, 82
  tributes, 83-4
Cheltenham Ladies College, 33, 52, 59
Chignell, Miss Ruth, 44, 48, 69-70
Clarke, Rear-Admiral Sir Philip, 113
Clifton, Miss, appointed 'Lady
  Governess', 19, 20, 29, 31

Drake House, 73
Donner, Sir Edward Bt., 73

Edinburgh, Admiral the Duke of (son
  of Queen Victoria), 31, 50
Edgerton, Miss Blanche, 94-5, 100, 101
Edgerton, Admiral the Hon. Sir
  Francis, 51
Edward VII, 15, 51
Elizabeth, Princess (as President), 105
Elizabeth, Queen (Coronation), 111
Elizabeth the Queen Mother, 112
Entrance examinations, 32-3

Falkland Islands, 60
Fayerman, Miss, 59, 62, 68
Fenn, Dr., 33, 38, 39
Fisher, Admiral Lord, 53
Fisher, The Rt. Hon. H. A. L., 69
Fraser, Admiral of the Fleet Lord, 108

George V, King, 51, 90
Girton College, Cambridge, 63, 70
Goodenough, Admiral Sir Wm.,
  94-5, 100, 102

Gordon House, 71
Gray, Dr. Oliver, 109
Grenville House, 71

Hall, Rear-Admiral Sir Arthur, 105, 113
Harris, Mrs. R., 87
High Rough, 99, 102
Holbrook, Miss M., 87, 96
  'Lady Black-out', 98, 103, 113
  Second Mistress, 115
  retirement, 116
Hood House, 75
Hope House (Richmond), 18, 25, 27
Hussey, Miss E., 76,
  Second Mistress, 78, 94
  war-time evacuation, 94-9
  character, 100, 103, 111

Jane Eyre (unsuitable for young
  mistresses), 43
Jellicoe, Admiral Sir John, 63
Julius, Dr., 21, 24, 33
Jutland, Battle of, 62

Kilmorey, Earl of, 26, 39

Leys, Miss Jemima, 40-1
  religious teaching, 47-8, 50, 52
  death, 78
'Lord Haw-Haw', 95

McClenaghan, Mrs Charlotte, 115
  Sixth Form House, 116, 117
  retirement, 118
Marina, Princess, 116
Marshall, Arthur (quoted), 91
Mary, Princess, marriage, 72
Mary, Queen, 72, 110
Maude, The Hon. Captain, 31
May, Princess (later Queen Mary), 51
Meux, Admiral Sir Hedworth, 60-1, 63
Milton, Dr. R., 109
Moody, Mollie, 64-5, 67, 95
Mountbatten of Burma, Admiral of
  the Fleet the Earl of, 73, 106, 117
Mowat, Miss A. A., Second Mistress, 75
  The Story of Education, 76, 78, 83
Mulgrave, Duchess of, 22
Mullens, J. A., 53-4, 71

Nelson House, 73
Northumberland, Duchess of, 16, 35

121

Oakley-Hill, Miss H. M., 9
  appointment, 84
  on use of leisure, 86, 88, 89
  wartime evacuation, 94-99, 100
  tributes to staff, 103
  new Kilmorey Block, 105, 109
  austerities, 110
  retirement, 113-4
Otter, Miss Diana, appointment, 118
  early achievements, 119
Osterberg, Madame Bergmann, 47

Parrat, Dr. Walter, 42

Queen Adelaide Fund, 36
Quinan, Miss, 31, 36, 39, 40

Reluctant Revolutionaries, 43
Royal Patriotic Fund, 26, 63
Royson, Samuel, 56

Shales, Mrs., 41, 47
Stemson, Mrs., 115
Stilwell, G. Holt, 78
Stoatley Hall, 99
Stone, Miss Helen (Mrs. Fowler),
  appointment as 'Lady Principal', 52,
  53, 54, 59, 68
Story of Education, The, 76

Thring, Dr. Edward, 43

Verdley Place (Fernhurst), 95-8
Victoria, Queen, 15, 48
Victory, The (School Magazine), 53,
  55, 60-1
Vulliamy, Lewis, 26

Williams, Admiral Sir Thomas, 15,
  16-18, 22, 25, 120